THE OFFICIAL PRICE GUIDE TO WICKER

®

BY
RICHARD SAUNDERS

FROM THE EDITORS
OF THE HOUSE OF COLLECTIBLES

THIRD EDITION
THE HOUSE OF COLLECTIBLES, NEW YORK, NEW YORK 10022

Important Notice. The format of *The Official Price Guide Series,* published by *The House of Collectibles,* is based on the following proprietary features: *All facts and prices are compiled through a nationwide sampling of information* obtained from noteworthy experts, auction houses, and specialized dealers. *Detailed "indexed" format* enables quick retrieval of information for positive identification. *Encapsulated histories* precede each category to acquaint the collector with the specific traits that are peculiar to that area of collecting. *Valuable collecting information* is provided for both the novice as well as the seasoned collector: How to begin a collection; how to buy, sell and trade; care and storage techniques; tips on restoration; grading guidelines; lists of periodicals, clubs, museums, auction houses, dealers, etc. *An average price range* takes geographic location and condition into consideration when reporting collector value. *An inventory checklist system* is provided for cataloging a collection.

All of the information, including valuations, in this book has been compiled from the most reliable sources, and every effort has been made to eliminate errors and questionable data. Nevertheless the possibility of error, in a work of such immense scope, always exists. The publisher will not be held responsible for losses which may occur in the purchase, sale, or other transaction of items because of information contained herein. Readers who feel they have discovered errors are invited to *write* and inform us, so they may be corrected in subsequent editions. Those seeking further information on the topics covered in this book are advised to refer to the complete line of Official Price Guides published by The House of Collectibles.

Published by: The House of Collectibles
202 East 50th Street
New York, New York 10022

Distributed by Ballantine Books, a division of Random House, Inc., New York and simultaneously in Canada by Random House of Canada Limited, Toronto.

Manufactured in the United States of America

Library of Congress Catalog Card Number: 82-82250

ISBN: 0-87637-248-5

10 9 8 7 6 5 4 3 2 1

TABLE OF CONTENTS

PREFACE

The prices quoted in this guide are based on average RETAIL prices for antique wicker furniture in good to excellent condition.

Because locality is a prime factor in determining prices for wicker furniture, I have attached a generous spread to the price ranges in this book in hopes that they will reflect the general nationwide average. Figures are based on estimates given to me over the past year by antique wicker specialty dealers from California to New York, Illinois to Florida. With this in mind, the reader should be aware of the fact that prices can fluctuate greatly from state to state and even from small towns to cities within a given state. However - as we will soon see - design, rarity, age, workmanship and overall condition play the biggest part in accurately pricing a piece of collectible wicker furniture.

If you wish to contact me with comments, additional information or additions for future editions of this book, please send a self-addressed stamped envelope with your letter to:

Richard Saunders
894 Laurel Avenue
Pacific Grove, California 93950

ACKNOWLEDGMENTS

My sincere thanks go out to the following antique wicker dealers and wicker restoration specialists. These individuals have graciously contributed photographs and valuable information: Judy Sikorski, Frank H. McNamee, Jim and Marion Redmond, Bill and Lee Stewart, Edith Langfur, Don Hays, Pamela Scurry, Frank Stagg, Dale Beebe, Forest Lightfoot, Hazel and Neil Terwilliger, Mike Bradbury, Ron and Lynn Youra, Charlotte and Steve Wagner, Jane Davis, Michon Gentray and Christa Carlson, Dr. Peter J. Isgrow, Sue Parker, Sandy Thatcher, Pat and Frank Allen, Joan Schiffer and Roz Gradinger, Lynn Cook and Morgan Schiffer, Vic and Anne Durkin, Henry and Maxine Spieske, Elizabeth and Richard King, Pam Thompson, Loren L. Lewis Jr., Sue Kaady, Kathy Glasglow, Tom Scheibal, Steve and Tammy Mottet, Alan Serebrin and Kathy Olin.

The following private collectors of antique wicker furniture have also contributed greatly to the quality of this book: Louise Olsson, Teri and Jan Gearhart, Nancy Waters, Mary Jean McLaughlin, Cheryl Wiese, James M. Shaffer, Jeanne Baggerly Ainsworth, Mrs. Thomas McDermott, Kathy James, Katherine Woodward Mellon, Mrs. Harvey Camins, Miss Margaret Hays, Mrs. Mary McNamee, Beverly Stephenson, John Hathaway and Mike York.

I would also like to thank the following individuals, institutions and general antique shops for their generous help: Carl Lugbauer, the Wakefield Historical Society, Barker Library (Harvard University), "Antiques World" magazine, Belli and Sabih, The Best of Everything, Toc of the Town, The Maison Bergerac Restaurant, The Wine Country Inn, Sandy Thatcher of The Finishing Touch and Robert Diamond of Maltman Enterprises.

PHOTOGRAPHS: Gary Denys, Dick Seidenzahl, Amy Lyons, Gene Komaromi, Pat Taylor, Jean Hagberg and John Dolan.

Special thanks go out to my wife, Paula, for her invaluable editorial assistance and loving encouragement.

PHOTOGRAPHIC RECOGNITION

Cover Photograph: Photographer — Marc Hudgeons, Orlando, FL 32809;
Courtesy of: Montgomery Auction Exchange, Route 17K, Montgomery, NY 12549.

NOTE TO READERS

MARKET REVIEW

The prices for collectible wicker have basically leveled off over the past two years. However, very fine and rare pieces are steadily increasing in value, especially those from the Victorian era. Last year, record prices were realized at auction for a Victorian Morris chair which brought $1,100 and a fancy Victorian square table which sold for $1,300.

Generally, wicker prices are the highest in Florida, New York, and Southern California. The best area overall for fine quality collectible wicker continues to be New England. This is due to the fact that the original wicker manufacturing industry in America was basically concentrated there. Vintage wicker from the 1920s is most plentiful in Florida.

Items to look for now include children's wicker and salesmen's samples which can still be found at reasonable prices. Finding salesmen's samples can present a bit of a challenge but the results can be most gratifying. These lovely pieces were scaled down replicas or models of full-size furniture and were carried by salesmen to demonstrate new lines. Now avidly sought by collectors for their unique charm, these delightful pieces are a valuable addition to any collection. Experts feel that prices for these pieces are bound to escalate in the coming years.

Another factor which has greatly contributed to the popularity of collectible wicker is the current design trend espousing the charming Victorian and "country" look in home decoration. These styles feature a return to the romanticism and comfort of a bygone era. New Victorian-style homes are being built today and are furnished with stained glass, lace curtains and wicker furniture. It is important to remember that vintage wicker is still a good buy when one considers the expense of new furniture. Certainly there is little comparison between the two in terms of charm and quality for the money spent. In the past, Victorian, Turn of the Century and Art Deco collectibles have been regarded with disdain among the elite corps of antique collectors. This has been due to the fact that objects from this period were often machine made and the antiques world has traditionally regarded anything so produced as being inherently inferior to handcrafted pieces. (This was not the case with wicker, however, which was, for the most part handmade.) In addition, these collectibles were regarded largely as curio pieces due to their size and elaborate style, and did not have the distinction of being old enough to qualify as a genuine antique. But time passed and new generations of collectors entered the marketplace looking for distinctive pieces at affordable prices. These young collectors were unable to afford the finest old pieces and did not like the new modern styles. What they did discover was that Victorian, Art Nouveau and Art Deco furnishings had charm, verve, uniqueness and durability and could be purchased inexpensively. While price may have been the determining factor in the beginning, this new design style soon took hold as more and more people were exposed to the delightful results. Also, the craftsmanship of these styles, which has largely been ignored for fifty years, became more and more evident to the public. Vintage wicker was the very core of this new school of design. Unlike the inferior reproduction wicker which has flooded the market, old wicker is very sturdy, having been built with solid hardwood frames. It is quite heavy compared to the poor quality oriental pieces imported today.

Collectible wicker is avidly sought by the most prestigious interior designers in the country for its quality and charm. Once viewed only as informal accent pieces, this furniture is found in every possible setting today from the most affluent, elegant homes right down to log cabins — and every economic strata in between. This wide acceptance of wicker is one of the most important considerations when assessing and projecting its market performance and potential. For while wicker may have its slow periods in terms of price increases, it is most unlikely that values will ever drop. Without a doubt, the values of fine wicker of the Victorian, Turn-of-the-Century and Art Deco periods will continue to climb.

INTRODUCTION

Airy. Open. Light. Fresh. These are just some of the words that come to mind when describing the elusive qualities of antique wicker furniture. Today the nostalgic look of handmade wicker has made it more popular than ever. Pieces from the 1860s to the 1920s are enjoying an unprecedented revival in popularity with the general public, antique dealers and interior designers. Wicker can possess an aura of Victorian elegance or conjure up memoirs of lazy summer days on a shady porch . . . simply put, it creates a mood.

Richard Saunders

Having stepped back into fashion within the last decade, fine wicker furniture is now poised for flight to a far higher level of popularity than ever before. While an 1881 article in "Scribner's" magazine described wicker as "capital stuff to fill up the gaps in the furnishing of a country house for the summer", today's eclectic style of decorating encourages the use of wicker to create a unique blend of informality and dimension to any room in the home and not simply "fill up the gaps." Furthermore, serious collectors and decorators alike are once again creating entire rooms of old wicker furniture — sunrooms, bedrooms, dining rooms — and the results are nothing less than fantastic.

The roots of this curious wicker renaissance have been traced to many sources. Some people claim that it began its comeback in the mid and late 1960s (after it had all but vanished from the scene in the early 1930s) when a younger generation began looking for "alternative" forms of furniture and happened across the then inexpensive wicker pieces at garage sales and flea markets. Justifiably, others point to its increased use by interior designers — the evidence of which can be seen by opening any home decorating magazine. Still others claim that the general public has, in an age of impersonal mass produced furniture, come to appreciate the fine craftsmanship that went into the making of wicker furniture. My own feeling is that the current wicker revival was brought about by a combination of these things . . . but the bottom line is that people are just beginning to realize that handmade wicker furniture is a true art form. Indeed, decorative arts museums across the country are finally taking wicker seriously and adding it to their collections.

One of the oldest surviving pieces of wicker furniture - an Egyptian wig chest (c. 1400 B.C.)
(Courtesy of the Cairo Museum).

The earliest piece of American wicker furniture came across the Atlantic on the Mayflower - a wicker cradle.
(Courtesy of the Pilgrim Hall Museum, Plymouth, Massachusetts).

By the time the Romans withdrew from their 1st century B.C. invasion of Britain in the 5th century, the British had inherited the concept of wickerwork furniture from the conquerors. Although the production of the wicker chair was little more than an extension of the basic basket-weaving techniques used in England for centuries, the British soon made these "twiggen" or "basket chairs" a staple during the Middle Ages. Eventually these crude wicker chairs evolved into a true "people's chair" and were made and used almost exclusively by English peasants.

Around the 16th century, wicker furniture was being made around the world. Countries enjoying warmer climates made use of rattan, cane, swamp reed and palm leaves, whereas, countries in cooler climates utilized rush, willow and wild grasses. Appropriately, the first piece of American wickerwork furniture arrived in the New World with the Pilgrims aboard the "Mayflower." Although there is still some confusion whether the wicker cradle used to rock Peregrine White to sleep on during that famous voyage across the Atlantic was of Dutch or Chinese origin, the fact remains that it is the earliest known piece of wicker furniture claimed by this country and holds and honored place at the Pilgrim Hall of Museum (see Photo).

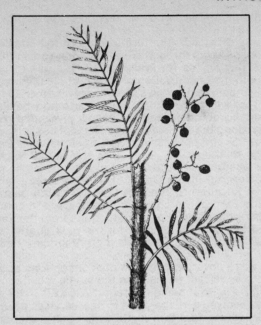

The rattan palm, from which cane and reed are derived, grows like a vine and can attain a height of six hundred feet. It thrives in the jungles of the Far East.

Wicker furniture can be traced back to ancient Egypt and, due to the dry atmosphere and air-tight tombs, it is here where some of the finest and oldest existing examples of wickerwork were discovered. As the logical outgrowth of a long standing basketry tradition (the Egyptians used local palm, wild grasses and swamp rush), larger utilitarian wickerwork items probably began appearing around 3000 B.C. Although the oldest piece of evidence of actual wickerwork furniture in existence is a stone statue of a Sumarian steward sitting on a wicker hassock (c. 2600 B.C.), it is the actual surviving pieces unearthed from tombs that have sparked the greatest scientific and public interest. Among these surviving wickerwork items are an exceptionally well-preserved toilet chest from the burial site of Queen Menutheotep at Thebes (c. 1600 B.C.) and several wicker stools and chests which were discovered in 1922 inside the tomb of King Tutankhamen (who met with an untimely death around 1325 B.C.) and is still known as the greatest archaeological discovery of all time. Last but not least, one of the finest and best preserved surviving wicker pieces from ancient Egypt is a wig chest (see photo) now housed at the Cairo Museum. Made of reed and papyrus around 1400 B.C., this piece was unearthed at the tomb of Yuia and Thuiu and has an interesting history. Following the custom of the day, lady Thuiu had her head shaved for hygienic reasons and thus had a very practical need for this wig chest. Note the construction of the piece — the joints are wrapped with reed for extra strength and the use of both horizontal and vertical wickerwork anticipates the "window" design often employed in wicker furniture of the 1910 to 1930 era . . . over 3000 years later!

The antiquity of wicker furniture from both the Greek and Roman civilizations is also known through stone carvings and, in the case of the Roman author Pliny (in his *Natural History),* the use of woven willow branches useful in the construction of those articles of luxury, reclining chairs. It is well known that willows were largely cultivated for use in the making of modest wicker furniture, horse carts and basketmaking. In fact, the ancient woven chair made of willow or swamp reed was constructed closely along the same lines of a piece of basketry, being woven in the same manner and possessing the same quality of flexibilty.

Importantly, it should be noted that the actual wicker furniture industry per se was born on American soil and not (as so many people still insist in believing) in the Orient. This widespread misconception might have been nurtured by the fact that the rattan palm (see photo) grows wild in the Far East. Also adding to the general confusion is the abundance of poor quality wicker reproductions from the Far East which have been imported into this country for the past quarter of a century. Ironically, these reproductions are based on American Victorian wicker designs.

Lastly, as we're covering common misconceptions about wicker in this chapter, it is important to mention the single most confusing point about this furniture — that being the term "WICKER". Not a material in itself, wicker has evolved over the years to now serve as an umbrella term which covers all woven furniture made from such materials as rattan, reed, cane, willow, fiber, rush, Oriental sea grass and other dried grasses (see "GLOSSARY" for details on all of these materials). Surprisingly, the word wicker (from the Swedish "wika", to bend, and "vikker', meaning willow) only came into widespread use after the turn-of-the-century. Before that time the old trade catalogues containing what we would now call wicker furniture were using the terms "rattan" or "reed" to describe their furniture.

MANUFACTURERS OF WICKER FURNITURE

During the early 1660s, in the opening years of the China trade by the East India Company, rattan began to be imported into England. However, it was not the rattan, but the glossy outer covering of this exotic palm (called cane) which was used extensively in weaving the backs and seats of wooden chairs. By the mid-18th century, Canton became the only port for foreign trade and, in time, both British and American traders became familiar with Chinese fanback and peacock chairs made from rattan and began bringing them home as objects of curiosity.

It was not until the early 1840s that four new ports of foreign trade opened up in China as a result of the Opium War. By this time it was common for clipper ships, sailing between these ports and America, to use whole rattan on board to prevent the cargo from shifting. And so it came to being dumped out on the Boston docks, a young grocer named Cyrus Wakefield became fascinated with the inherent possibilities of these odd-looking flexible poles. He soon joined a group of volunteers who were carting the material off the docks and decided to take some of the rattan home and conducted an experiment by wrapping an ordinary wooden rocking chair with the strange material. From this humble beginning Wakefield (destined to become the father of the American wicker furniture industry) conducted increasingly elaborate experiments with rattan and became so obsessed with the possibilities of the material that he soon sold his grocery business to his brother and decided to embark on a jobbing trade in rattan. After selling his first bulk purchase to basket makers and furniture companies (who utilized the cane for weaving chair seats), his Horatio Alger-type success story was put into motion. Within a few years his cane was in such great demand by furniture manufacturers that he was forced to hire workers in Canton, China, to hand-strip the cane from the whole rattan. Business-wise this proved to be the difference. The cheap labor in Canton allowed him to hire his own clipper ships to import the popular cane at a fraction of the cost.

During these early years Wakefield led a double life — that of rattan jobber and furniture designer. Although his rattan furniture was still in the experimental stage, he continued in earnest with innovative designs until he and his wife moved to South Reading, Massachusetts, in 1955, where they established the Wakefield Rattan Company along with rushing Mill River. At this point furniture production took the upper hand and never relinquished its position. Now not only were whole rattan and cane utilized in the making of his wicker furniture but "reed" (the inner pith of whole rattan which, up until this time, was treated as waste) was found to be superior to rattan due to its greater flexibility and therefore lent itself to the growing popularity of ornate Victorian designs.

Through the 1860s the Wakefield Rattan Company grew tremendously and virtually cornered the market on wicker furniture. Indeed, Cyrus Wakefield became a rich man and after donating more than $120,000 to South Reading for the purpose of constructing a new town hall the local citizenry voted to change the name of their town to honor him and, in 1868, renamed their town Wakefield, Massachusetts.

A few years before his death in 1873, Cyrus Wakefield began selling whole rattan to Levi Heywood, founder of Heywood Brothers Company of Gardner, Massachusetts — the largest wood chair manufacturer in the United States. Established in 1826, Heywood Brothers and company was known for its Windsor and bentwood chairs — the latter product being highly praised by no one less than Francis Thonet of Vienna, son of the creator of the famous bentwood rocker. With this in mind, it's not hard to see why Levi Heywood kept close tabs on the Wakefield Rattan Company and he began producing his own wicker furniture shortly after the Civil War. Furthermore, Heywood Brothers and Company had in their employ a certain inventor named Gardner A. Watkins who not only invented a loom that could weave cane into continuous sheets but also devised an automatic channeling machine which cut a groove around a wooden chair seat. When these two inventions were combined and put to use the results were dramatic. No longer were hand-caners hired to weave seats. The age of pre-woven or "set-in" cane seats (fastened to the framework by means of a triangular-shaped reed called "spline") proved to be much more economical than hand-caning. With these substan-

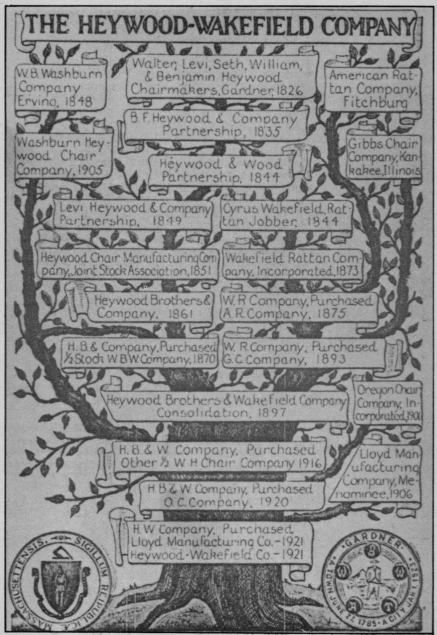

This Heywood-Wakefield "family tree" accurately follows the various origins of each side of the famous company.
(From "The Five Heywood Brothers" by Richard N. Green).

tial savings in labor costs, Levi Heywood was able to enter into the field of wicker furniture production whole heartedly and for the next quarter of a century the Wakefield Rattan Company (now headed by Cyrus Wakefield II, Mr. Wakefield's nephew and namesake) and Heywood Brothers and Company (headed by Henry Heywood after the death of his uncle, Levi Heywood, in 1882) became fierce competitors.

Although the competitiveness between the two major companies was keen during these years, it was the general wicker-buying public who ultimately benefited — for improved designs and lowered prices were the end result of this famous inner-industry rivalry. Yet, surprisingly, in April of 1897 the two titans decided to merge and formed the "Heywood Brothers and Wakefield Company", a consolidation which all but monopolized the quality wicker furniture industry from the turn-of-the-century through the 1920s. During this period the newly-formed company pooled the top line of craftsmen, designers and business minds from both companies and came up with the cream of the crop in all three fields.

In the early 1900s public taste veered toward simple, straight-lined designs in furniture and away from what was then considered to be the overly-ornate, gauche designs of the Victorian age. Since wicker was seen as one of the chief perpetrators many fine pieces were hauled to the dump or simply burned. Like any successful business, Heywood

Cyrus Wakefield (1811-1873), the Boston grocer who became the father of the American Wicker furniture industry.
(Courtesy of the Wakefield Historical Society).

Brothers and Wakefield Company began altering their designs to conform to the public taste and, around 1910, began designing wicker in the popular Mission style. However, in the years to follow rising labor costs proved to be a considerable problem and it wasn't until 1917 that Marshall B. Lloyd of Menominee, Michigan, invented a machine to weave man-made fiber of chemically treated twisted paper which could then be transferred directly from his patented "Lloyd loom' and fitted directly onto the awaiting frames. This "art fiber" furniture caught on quickly — it not only conformed to the existing penchant for simple designs in furniture but also offered these pieces at a substantial savings when compared to the hand-woven reed designs of the same era.

Recognizing that the public had preferred the closely woven style of wicker furniture since the early 1900s and knowing that the Lloyd loom would cut both labor and material costs while at the same time produce the desired style of wicker, the Heywood Brothers and Wakefield Company purchased the Lloyd Manufacturing Company in 1921. Not only did they readily accept the concept of mass production, the giant company marked the occasion by further simplifying its official corporate title to the "Heywood-Wakefield Company". Unfortunately, this seemingly wise business move proved to be the beginning of the end for the wicker furniture industry. After an initial surge of popularity, machine-made wicker, along with the entire industry, hit the dust in the early 1930s. Using a considerable amount of hindsight, it's not hard to see that the strongest tie between wicker furniture and the American public was the fact that it was handmade from natural materials. When the machine age entered into the picture and made use of the Lloyd loom and man-made fiber the true "art" of wicker furniture was lost in the transition.

After 1930 the Heywood-Wakefield Company managed to keep up with the times by manufacturing wood and metal furniture. However, the Gardner, Massachusetts plant was forced to close down its wood furniture production in 1979, and now the only branch of the company that is actively involved in producing furniture (auditorium seating, metal outdoor furniture and school furniture) is located in Menominee, Michigan. Ironically, the home of Marshall B. Lloyd, the man who inadvertently brought about the downfall of the wicker furniture industry with his mechanical loom!

The full effects of the recent foreclosure of the Gardner plant in Massachusetts is just now being felt by true wicker buffs. As late as the 1970s Carl Lugbauer, the dedicated company historian, was accepting photographs of wicker from the public and (if these pieces carried labels with the names "Heywood" of "Wakefield" on them) researched the origins of the specific designs as a special service. Mr. Lugbauer's research would usually lead him to the company's archives of old trade catalogues (going back to the 1850s) and he was so painstakingly accurate in pinpointing the earliest dates of specific designs that the company began issuing official "Certificates of Authenticity" to the owner. Although it was a special service of the company, Mr. Lugbauer retired in 1976 and, regrettably, the historical consciousness of the Heywood-Wakefield Company seems to have retired with him.

The following lists wicker furniture manufacturers and retailers who were in business between 1840 and 1930, and has been compiled by the author and supplemented by over thirty wicker restoration specialists and antique dealers who specialize in wicker furniture. The vast majority of the company labels were attached to the bottom or the back of the seat and were made of paper, metal or celluloid:

A

Acme Company
(Chicago, Illinois)

Adams Furniture Company
(Toronto, Canada)
1910-1930's

American Rattan Company
(Fitchburg, Massachusetts)
Purchased by the Wakefield
Rattan Company in 1875.

American Fibre Company
(Sheboygan, Wisconsin)

American Reedcraft Corporation
(New York, New York)

Art Rattan Works
(Oakland, California)

B

Baltimore Wicker and Carriage Company
(Baltimore, Maryland)

Baumgarten

J. & C. Berrian
(New York, New York)
One of the earliest manufacturers of wicker furniture.

Bielecky Brothers, Inc.
(New York, New York)
Established around 1900 and still in operation.

Blindcraft

Bloch Go-Cart Company
(Philadelphia, Pennsylvania)
Established in 1897. According to Miriam Bloch Simon, granddaughter of the founder of this fine company, her grandfather designed the first hooded stroller as well as the first drop-footwell stroller. The showroom was in Philadelphia while the factory was in Egg Harbor, New Jersey.

Bloomingdale Brothers
(New York, New York)

The Bolton Willow Shop
(Cambridge, Massachusetts)

Boston Willow Furniture
(Boston, Massachusetts)

Walter J. Brennan Company
(New York, New York)

Brighton Furniture Company
(Island Pond, Vermont)

Bungalow-Homecraft Furniture

C

Cane-Craft
(New York, New York)

Chicago Reedware Manufacturing Company
(Chicago, Illinois)

China Sea Grass Furniture & Rugs

Chittenden-Eastman Company
(Burlington, Iowa)
A major wicker furniture manufacturer with a much deserved reputation for making fine Victorian and turn-of-the-century wicker.

John A. Colby & Son
(Chicago, Illinois)

The Colson Chair Company
(Elyria, Ohio)

Colt Willow Ware Works
(Hartford, Connecticut)
1850's-1873.

Craftsman Furniture
(Eastwood, New York)
Gustav Stickley's Company.
Established in 1898.

A. Cummings
(New York, New York)

Cunningham Reed and Rattan Company
(New York, New York)
Established in 1919.

D

F. Debski
(New York, New York)

P. Derby & Company
(Gardner, Massachusetts)

J.A. Dickerman and Company

Downing Carriage Company
(Erie, Pennsylvania)

Dryad Works
(Leicester, England)
Established in 1907 by Charles and Albert Crampton, members of an old and highly-respected British basket-making family. England's finest "cane furniture" came from this company. Like some Oriental imports of this period, Dryan wicker furniture was made without the use of nails or tacks. It was imported exclusively by "W. & J. Sloane" of New York City and made from locally-grown willow.

F

Ficks Reed Company
(New York, New York)
Established in 1928.

Ford-Johnson Fibre Rush Furniture
(Michigan City, Indiana)

G

Gendron Iron Wheel Company
(Toledo, Ohio)
Established 1873. Specialized in wicker carriages.

Gibbs Chair Company
(Kankakee, Illinois)
Purchased by Wakefield Rattan Company in 1893.

The Grand Central Wicker Shop
(New York, New York)
Established around 1910.

Grand Rapids Fiber Cord Company
(Grand Rapids, Michigan)

H

Hartford Chair Company
(Hartford, Connecticut)

Hedstrom Union Company
(Gardner, Massachusetts)

Heywood Brothers and Company
(Gardner, Massachusetts)
1868-1897.

Heywood Brothers and Wakefield Company
(Gardner, Massachusetts)
1897-1921.

Heywood-Wakefield Company
(Gardner, Massachusetts)
Established in 1921.

Walter Heywood Chair Company
(New York, New York)

GENUINE REED FURNITURE

Evercharm

1925

1928

Heywood-Morrill Rattan Company
(Gardner, Massachusetts)
1870's to 1897.

Dean Hicks

High Point Bending and Chair Company
(Silver City, North Carolina)
Established in 1921. Makers of quality fiber furniture.

Huntingdon Rattan & Reed Company

J

Jenkins-Phipps
(Wakefield, Massachusetts)
1905-1912.

Johnson-Randall Company
(Traverse City, Michigan)

Jones-Smith
(New York, New York)

K

Kaltex Furniture Company
(Jackson, Michigan)

Karpen Brothers

Karpen Guaranteed Construction Furniture
(Chicago, Michigan City, New York)

Kelly Brothers
(Gardner, Massachusetts)

The Kinley Manufacturing Company
(Chicago, Illinois)

L

The Larkin Company
(Buffalo, New York)

Larkins & Company
(San Francisco, California)
Established 1862.

Leader

Lloyd Manufacturing Company
(Menominee, Michigan)
1906-1921. Purchased by Heywood Brothers and Company in 1921.

Long Beach Reed & Willow Furniture Company
(New York, New York)

The Luburg Manufacturing Company
(Philadelphia, Pennsylvania)

M

Madewell Chair Company
(Sheboygan, Wisconsin)

Madison Basketcraft Company
(Burlington, Iowa)

Manhattan Wicker Company
(New York, New York)

Mastercraft Reed Company

McGibbon & Company
(New York, New York)

Joseph P. McHugh & Company
(New York, New York)
Established in 1878. Heywood-Wakefield Company's strongest competition in the 1920's. Quality handmade reed furniture with an emphasis on unique and custom-made designs.

A. Meinecke & Son
(Milwaukee, Wisconsin)

Mentzer Reed Company
(Grand Rapids, Michigan)

Lloyd Loom Furniture, with its flawlessly smooth fabric, is woven by the patented Lloyd Loom method. Ask your dealer to show you this handsome furniture, or send for booklet

One unbroken strand of fine wicker is *spirally woven* on the famous *Lloyd Loom* to form the graceful, seamless *Lloyd Loom* Carriage. No other carriage has this spiral weaving

No carriage offers greater value than this

Search the town over. You will not find any other baby carriage with the features which the *Lloyd Loom* Carriage offers for a price as low. *Spiral weaving* makes this lovely carriage distinctive in design and in price.

The graceful, bowl-shaped body, with its smooth surface unmarred by seams, corners, or pieced short ends, is obtained by *spiral weaving*. The many refinements of finish, the exclusive Lloyd conveniences, are made

possible by the low production cost of *spiral weaving*. Steel-centered upright stakes used exclusively in all Lloyd products add great strength.

If you don't know where to find *Lloyd Loom* Carriages, write us for the dealer's name and our interesting booklet.

THE LLOYD MANUFACTURING COMPANY
(Heywood-Wakefield Co.)
Dept. 2-242, Menominee, Mich.
Canadian Factory: Orillia, Ont.

Patent Process
Lloyd
LOOM WOVEN
Baby Carriages & Furniture

1925

**Merikord · American Chair
Company**
(Sheboygan, Wisconsin)

Metropolitan Chair Company
(Hartford, Connecticut)

**Midland Chair and Seating
Company**
(Michigan City, Indiana)
Successors to the "Ford-
Johnson Company".

Minnet & Company

Montgomery Ward Company
Retail sales of wicker since the
1880's. Bought wicker wholesale
from various mid-sized companies
since the 1880's and built up an inexpensive line of wicker furniture
offered through their famous mail-
order catalogues.

Murphy of Michigan
(Gardner, Massachusetts)

N

N.E.P. Company
(Boston, Massachusetts)

Newburgh Reed Company
(Newburgh, New York)

New England Chair Company
(Hartford, Connecticut)

New England Reed Company
(Boston, Massachusetts)

New York State House of Refuge
(New York, New York)
Established in the 1850's.

New Haven Chair Company
(New Haven, Connecticut)
Established in the 1890's.

Niagra Reed Company
(Buffalo, New York)

M. A. Nicolai
(Dresden, Germany)
Turn-of-the-century wicker manufacturer which was among the
first to use straight-lined designs.

Northfield Furniture Company
(Sheboygan, Wisconsin)

Novelty Rattan Company
(Boston, Massachusetts)

O

A. H. Ordway and Company
(South Framingham,
Massachusetts)

Oregon Chair Company
Incorporated in 1906. Purchased
by Heywood Brothers and Company in 1920.

P

Pacific Coast Rattan Company
(San Francisco and Oakland,
California)

Paine's Furniture Company
(Boston, Massachusetts)
According to Richard Green-
wood, former president of the
Heywood-Wakefield Company,
Paine's Furniture had all of their
wicker made on a special order
basis by Heywood Brothers and
Wakefield Company.

Peabody & Whitney

Peck & Hills
(New York, New York)

Piaget-Donnelly Company
(Grand Rapids, Michigan)
Importers of wicker made in
China after 1910.

Pioneer

Prairie Grass Furniture Company, Inc.
(Glendale, Long Island, New York)

The Puritan Company
(Gardner, Massachusetts)

R

G. W. Randall & Company
(Grand Rapids, Michigan)
One of the chief companies that sold wholesale wicker furniture to "Sears, Roebuck & Company".

The Reed Shop

Reedcraft Furniture Company
(Chicago - Los Angeles)
Early 1900's to 1920's.

Reedcraft, Inc.
(Baldsinsville, Massachusetts)

Reedfibre
(Iona, Michigan)

The Bemis Riddell Fibre Company
(Sheboygan, Wisconsin)

Rustic Hickory Company
Established in 1913.

S

Sargent Manufacturing Company
(Chicago, Illinois)

Schober & Company
(Philadelphia, Pennsylvania)
Established in 1892.

Sears, Roebuck & Company
(Chicago, Illinois)
Retail sales of wicker furniture since the 1880's. Bought wicker wholesale from various mid-sized companies since the 1880's and built up an inexpensive line of wicker. Their main concern was to undercut the competition and thus the overall quality of their pieces often suffered.

Sheboygan Reed and Fibre Furniture Company
(Sheboygan, Wisconsin)
One of the few companies known to make wicker salesmen's samples during the 1920's.

W. & J. Sloane
(New York, New York)
Exclusive importers of "Dryad" English Cane Furniture.

Spear & Company
(Pittsburgh, Pennsylvania)

The Gustav Stickley Company
(Eastwood, New York)
Established in 1898.

Stickley-Brandt Furniture Company
(Binghamton, New York)

Sunreed-Horace Mills Ltd.
(Newark-on-Trent, England)

T

A. A. Tisdale & Company
(Leominster, Massachusetts)

Topf & Company
(New York, New York)

Tung Mow Furniture Company
(Hong Kong)

U

Uhran Carriage Company
(Rochester, New York)

V

Valley City Rattan Company
(Grand Rapids, Michigan)

J. B. Van Shriver Company
(Camden, New Jersey)

A. A. Vantine & Company, Inc.
(New York, New York)
Importers of fine wicker from Canton, China, since the early 1900's.

Vollmer/Prag-Rudmiker
(Vienna, Austria)
Established around 1900.

W

Wakefield Rattan Company
Wakefield and Boston, (Massachusetts)
Established in 1855. Incorporated in 1873.

John Wanamaker
(Philadelphia, Pennsylvania)

Washburn-Heywood Chair Company
(Boston, Massachusetts)
Established 1905. Purchased by Heywood Brothers and Wakefield Company in 1916.

W. B. Washburn Company
(Erving, Massachusetts)

Whitney Reed Chair Company
(Leominster, Massachusetts)

F. A. Whitney Carriage Company
(Leominster, Massachusetts)

W. F. Whitney & Company
(South Ashburnham, Massachusetts)

Wicker-Kraft Company
(Newburgh, New York)

Willow & Reed
(Brooklyn, New York)
Established in 1923. According to the president of "Willow & Reed", Henry Olka, this was one of the chief companies that sold wicker wholesale to both "Sears, Roebuck & Company" and "Montgomery Ward Company" during the 1920's.

Willowcraft
(Cambridge, Masschusetts)

Y

Ypsilanti Reed Furniture Company
(Ionia, Michigan)

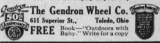

furniture is equally adapted to both the summer and winter home.

Its artistic qualities and great durability have won for Willowcraft its reputation as the best willow furniture obtainable. Avoid cheap imitations of the genuine Willowcraft.

Our free catalog offers 165 splendid suggestions.

The Willowcraft Shops

Box C   North Cambridge, Mass.

1913

F OR half a century mothers everywhere have recognized the master craftsmanship in Gendron baby vehicles. Care and precision in workmanship, highest grade of material have made Gendron the standard cab of the world.

Artillery, ball bearing wheels assure ease of running. Deep cushions and upholstery of soft, fine texture are comfortable for baby. Gendron carriages only are equipped with the famous Marshall spring upholstery. Beauty of design and delicately colored finish make for the true luxury and refinement that is so evident in every Gendron model.

And back of these splendid features is the sturdy built-in quality of fifty years' experience.

The best dealers everywhere sell the complete Gendron line. See the display in your city.

The Gendron Wheel Co.
611 Superior St.,   Toledo, Ohio
FREE Book—"Outdoors with Baby." Write for a copy

1914

Oriole Go-Basket

Reclining Model

Can be used from time of birth. It is a combined Go-Cart, High Chair, Jumper and Bassinet. Can be shifted instantly into three positions. You can take baby *anywhere* in an Oriole. Where impossible to wheel, it can be changed to a carrier without removing baby. Lightest perambulator made. Long, flexible springs prevent all jolts and jars.

Convenient for mother and baby. Ask your dealer. Look for the name — avoid imitations. If he doesn't carry it, write us for catalogue.

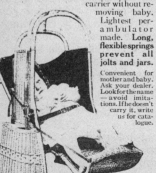

THE WITHROW MFG. CO.
2602 Spring Grove Ave., Cincinnati, O.

1915

Special

Summer

Offer

Complete with seat and back cushions in
denim or cretonne, - - - - - $7.25
Stained any color, - - - - - - 1.00
F. O. B. New York.

During this summer only we offer this strong, comfortable Arm Chair at this special price, to impress our new address on the minds of our friends, and to acquaint those whom we wish to make our friends, with the high quality of our HAND WROUGHT WILLOW WARE.

We also make a specialty of interior decoration and upholstery.

Sketch of willow pieces in large diversity of styles on request.

WALTER J. BRENNAN COMPANY
14 East 47th Street   New York City
Formerly 437 Lexington Ave.

1915

WHERE TO FIND WICKER FURNITURE TODAY

As we have seen in the preceding list of wicker furniture manufacturers from the past, most companies were located in the east, midwest and northern states and, even in this mobile society, that's where the majority of it remains. Yet, wherever you live, the fact that people are "getting wise" to antique wicker furniture cannot be overlooked. Generally speaking, the days of finding old wicker stored in attics or barns is over. If Aunt Mildred didn't know that her wicker was worth something five years ago you can almost bet that friends have set her straight by now or offered to buy it up themselves. Of course, if you hustle and luck is on your side you can still come across a real bargain now and then (especially if you can find a damaged piece which is repairable) and that's where a good deal of the appeal of wicker collecting lies. Unfortunately today it's a lot like prospecting for gold, and sections of the country that were once rich in wicker deposits seem to be playing out at an alarming rate.

If you're just starting to collect wicker, the best thing you can do is to let friends, relatives and antique dealers know about your new interest. The more "feelers" you have out the more likely you are to find something. Also check your local thrift shops and hit some garage sales. However, before you jump at what you think is a bargain you should study this book carefully as well as visit some wicker specialty shops so you know what quality antique wicker looks like. Once you have a feel for wicker you might want to try going to some flea markets . . . but again, the last word here is "know your wicker". I can't emphasize this enough because many flea market sellers are simply not knowledgeable in this admittedly specialized field and will put "antique" prices on 1960-1970 wicker reproductions. By the same token, if you know the value of antique wicker and know how to spot it, you'll have the upper hand when that weekend dealer offers a piece of antique wicker at a fraction of the going price.

Antique shows can also be a good source to find good quality wicker, and to partake in an interesting interchange of knowledge with dealers. With tickets running between $1.50 and $3.50 you can hardly go wrong and you'll usually walk out of a show knowing more than you did when you came in. Another good point about shows is that they can accommodate anywhere from 50 to 250 booths under one roof and therefore give the potential buyer a huge selection of items. You should also realize that most of the dealers at shows own shops, and that they probably have more wicker furniture which they simply did not have room to take along.

Buying wicker from antique shops that carry a general line of antiques can also unearth good bargains from time to time. Although most antique dealers will bargain with you on any given item, many refuse to budge on their prices and it's ultimately up to the buyer to know what is overpriced. Bargaining can be especially effective when buying more than one piece, that is, assuming you make a realistic offer.

Antique auctions can also turn up some good deals in wicker but the prospective buyer should thoroughly examine the merchandise at the auction preview. A few points to check would be the structure and overall condition of the piece (all auction items are sold on an "as is" basis), the existence of paper or metal labels which identify the manufacturer, the uniqueness of the design and, of course, the comfort of the piece. These previews not only allow the public to examine the wicker but also give you the advantage of making a calm decision as to what you are willing to pay before you are carried away by the contagious excitement generated at most auctions. In fact, a good way to arrive at your top figure for a given piece of wicker would be to go through the photos in this price guide and pick the piece which most resembles the one at the auction. Once you locate something similar in design and age, I would say that the price range quoted would be a reliable barometer on todays market, and I would strongly recommend that you stop your bidding if the price climbs 20% above the highest listed price.

Although some general antique auctions might periodically carry a sparse amount of wicker furniture, there are two annual auctions that specialize in antique wicker:

Montgomery Auction Exchange
Route 17 K
Montgomery, New York 12549

Over the past decade owner Ralph Losinno has turned his wicker auction into a gala event in the world of wicker. Some of the finest wicker in the country changes hands here in the first week of April every year. Write Mr. Losinno for specific dates and other details or call (914) 457-9549.

John C. Roselle Co.
Commercial Drive
Lakeville, Massachusetts 02346

Mr. Roselle's wicker auction is the second largest in the United States and is filled with quality antique wicker. The auction takes place each March. Call (617) 947-2122 for further details.

ANTIQUE DEALERS WHO SPECIALIZE IN WICKER FURNITURE

To further illustrate that we live in an age of specialization, the following section will deal entirely with antique shops that specialize in wicker furniture. These wicker shops are your best bet when it comes to finding a large selection of quality antique wicker. The owners of these specialty shops have a good deal of expertise in the field and can answer questions about wicker as well as add your name and phone number to their "want lists" if you are looking for a specific piece they don't have in stock. Often the best places to buy antique wicker, the owners have chosen their merchandise with an eye for overall beauty, quality of construction and materials, design and rarity.

I have added comments about those shops which I have either visited or about which I have firsthand knowledge.

ALABAMA

Allen's Antiques & Collectibles
121 Telegraph Road
Chickasaw, Alabama 33611
Pat and Frank Allen have been selling quality antique wicker out of their charming specialty shop for the past six years.

ARIZONA

The Seat Weaving Shop
Two locations:
2214 North 24th Street
Phoenix, Arizona 85008

7223 East 2nd Street
Scottsdale, Arizona 85251
Owner Lynn Cook is justifiably proud of her beautiful wicker shop. With a good eye for fine pieces and the help of three partners, she opened a satellite shop in Scottsdale.

CALIFORNIA

The Hays House of Wicker
Two locations:
1730 East Walnut
Pasadena, California 91106

8565 Melrose Avenue
Beverly Hills, California 90069
One of the top wicker dealers in the country, owner Don Hays has expanded his original Pasadena shop to include Beverly Hills. Both of his California shops carry the very best in antique and custom-made new wicker furniture. He travels extensively in search of the rare and unusual in antique wicker. Everything is top quality. In-house restoration. He also rents out wicker for television and movie productions.

Lightfoot House
8259 Melrose Avenue
Los Angeles, California 90046
A pioneer in the antique wicker revival, owner Dale Beebe began selling and restoring wicker in 1965. His sizable inventory is still among the finest in the country. The emphasis is on rarity and quality. He also rents out antique wicker to numerous movie productions as well as television programs.

Wisteria Antiques
2600 Soquel Avenue
Santa Cruz, California 95062
Owners Michael Schwartz and Christa Carlson are former New Yorkers who have a fine eye for quality antique wicker and travel the country for unique pieces. The shop is large and well-stocked. Custom upholstery also done on the premises. Wisteria also offers expert interior decoration services with an emphasis on wicker.

House of Wicker
870 Valencia
San Francisco, California 94110
Owner Frank Stagg is one of the earliest antique wicker specialty dealers in the country and an authority on the subject. Although he has cut down on his wicker inventory in the past few years, his shop is still a hotbed for unique and rare antique wicker. Nothing but the best here.

Carol Dimond Antiques
Located in The Pavilion
610 Sir Frances Drake Blvd.
San Anselmo, California 94960
Carol Dimond has been selling quality antique wicker out of her beautiful Marin County shop for the past four years.

Isgrow & Company
1125 Soquel Avenue
Santa Cruz, California 95062
Owner Dr. Peter J. Isgrow has a large selection of fine antique wicker and also does expert in-house restoration. A quality shop throughout.

Serendipity
108 F. Street
Eureka, California 95501
Hooper and Griffith's "Serendipity" is a charming wicker shop located in Eureka's historic "Old Town." A top quality shop throughout.

Bale Mill Inn & Antiques
3431 North St. Helena Highway
St. Helena, California 94574
    Owner Tom Scheibal not only runs an interesting antique shop (with an emphasis on wicker) but also features a beautiful Inn atop his shop which is furnished with antique wicker. Located in the heart of California's majestic wine country.

Arabesque Antiques
417 Trout Gulch Road
Aptos, California 95003
    Owners Steve and Tammy Mottet are long-time collectors and really know their wicker. Their spacious shop is usually well-stocked with fine antique wicker.

The Finishing Touch
5636 College Avenue
Oakland, California 94618
    A gifted repair person, owner Sue Parker began restoring wicker in 1974 and in 1980 expanded her service shop to sell her own carefully restored pieces. This charming shop with its warm, friendly atmosphere offers an eclectic collection of wicker ranging from fine Victorian pieces to Bar Harbor wicker to quality new pieces.

The Wicker Warehouse
965 West Second
Pomona, California 91766

CONNECTICUT

A Summer Place
29 Whitfield Street
Guilford, Connecticut 06437
    Mary Jane McLaughlin's wicker specialty shop is now celebrating its second year in business and is causing a tremendous stir in the world of wicker. Her 200-plus piece inventory includes some of the most rare and sought after pieces in the country, and her 400 piece warehouse is truly amazing. The largest private collector in the country, McLaughlin's shop reflects her selectivity and expert eye for wicker. Her new shop is a must see for collectors and dealers alike. Her specialty is museum-quality Victorian wicker although

she carries pieces from all collectible eras. She is also highly respected for working closely and successfully with interior designers. Call her for more information at (203) 453-5153.

Connecticut Antique Wicker
1052 Rear Main Street
Newington, Connecticut
    Owners Henry and Maxine Spieske have an extensive (and professionally restored) selection of fine antique wicker. Their two-room shop is a treasure-hunters dream. All pieces repaired and refinished by Henry, who is regarded as the top wicker restoration specialist in the country.

Todburn Antiques
Post Road
Westport, Connecticut 06880

Priscilla Furniture, Inc.
355 Post Road
Darien, Connecticut 06820

DELAWARE

Seaport Antiques
Route 54
Fenwick, Delaware 19975

FLORIDA

Frantiques Antique Wicker
1109½ West Waters Avenue
Tampa, Florida 33604
    Owner Fran Watts is the most knowledgeable wicker dealer in Florida. Her large shop is full of rare and unique wicker. In-house repair also available.

Antiques & Wicker Sales
1425 W. Busch Blvd.
Tampa, Florida 33612
    Owner Mary Wilfong specializes in antique Victorian and casual wicker. In business for the past eight years, Mary is a very knowledgeable dealer and consistently comes up with quality pieces.

Antique Wicker
5150 S.W. 60th Place
Miami, Florida 33155
    Owner Kathy Bondhus specializes in Victorian and Art Deco wicker. Her 500 piece inventory is a real eye-opener.

Den of Antiquity
831-B N. Federal Hwy.
Ft. Lauderdale, Florida 33304

Garrison Antiques
1210 North Federal Highway
Delray Beach, Florida 33444

Hambrick House Antique Wicker
835 Highway 17
Orange Park, Florida

The Willow Tree
376 South County Rd.
Palm Beach, Florida 33480
    Owner Greta Sones opened this interesting wicker specialty shop in South Florida last year, although she has been a private collector for the past fifteen years and has sold wicker out of her Newton, Massachusetts shop for the past decade. Over 100 pieces in stock at all times. All wicker restored to perfection. Open in season.

Victorian House of Wicker
920 E. Las Olas Blvd.
Fort Lauderdale, Florida
(305) 467-6867
    Extensive selection, over 200 Victorian pieces on display at all times.

GEORGIA

Heirloom Wicker
Cates Center
110 E. Andrews Drive, N. W.
Atlanta, Georgia 30305
    Owners Gail Dearing and Jeanne Barlow have been offering quality antique wicker out of this shop for the past three years. A fine selection and in-house repair. 100-150 quality pieces in stock at all times.

Wickerwill Antiques
5485 Peachtree Road
Chamblee, Georgia 30341

ILLINOIS

The Collected Works
905 Ridge Road
Wilmette, Illinois 60091
    Owners Bill and Lee Stewart are true authorities in the field. Both private collectors and dealers, they have a keen appreciation for quality antique wicker. Some of the finest pieces in the entire country can be seen at their beautiful shop and all are restored to perfection by the owners.

Calendar Court Antiques
108 Calendar Court
La Grange, Illinois 60525

The Wicker Witch of Chicago
2146 West Belmont
Chicago, Illinois 60618

Wicker & Feathers
804 Main Street
Peoria, Illinois 61602

INDIANA

The Yellow Wagon
400 West Melbourne
Logansport, Indiana 46947

Wicker & Things
2002 Broadway
Fort Wayne, Indiana 46804

IOWA

Wilson's Wicker and Weaving
1509 Main Street
Cedar Falls, Iowa 50613

KENTUCKY

The Red Brick House
120 East Main
Midway, Kentucky 40347

LOUSIANA

The Wicker Gazebo
3137 Magazine Street
New Orleans, Louisiana 70115
Owners Harry Bale and Ken Kirkwood have a huge two-story showroom of wicker furniture. Although they carry 10% antique and 90% mid-to-high quality reproductions, their inventory is nevertheless impressive. The owners feel that antique wicker is too hard to find in this area and have (over the past five years) concentrated on reproduction imports from the Phillippines, Hong Kong and mainland China. Their antique stock, although limited, is always of good quality.

MAINE

Antique Wicker
Main Street
Northeast Harbor, Maine 04662
Owners Elizabeth and Richard King are experts in the field and offer a wide selection of completely restored antique wicker.

Oxbow Farm Antiques
Route 1
Lincolnville Beach, Maine 04849

MARYLAND

The Wicker Lady of Maryland
505 Jumpers Hole Road
Severna Park, Maryland 21146
Owners Linda and Gary Koch have specialized in antique wicker for the past five years. They have a 150-200 piece stock at all times.

Joan M. Cole Wicker
P.O. Box 34150
Bethesda, Maryland 20817
Call (301) 983-1805 for appointment
Joan Cole has specialized in selling quality antique wicker for 12 years and always has between 160 and 225 pieces in stock. An avid collector herself, she travels extensively to find rare pieces. All her wicker is professionally restored before it is offered to the public.

Whippee's Wicker
523 Herring Avenue
Fairhaven, Maryland 20754

MASSACHUSETTS

The Wicker Porch
Route 28
Cranberry Highway
Wareham, Massachusetts 02571
Owner Frank H. McNamee runs one of the finest antique wicker shops in the country. A highly-qualified expert in the field, he's situated in the heart of "Heywood-Wakefield" country and has a keen eye for fine wicker. Top-quality in-house restoration. His shop is filled with excellent antique wicker and is usually filled with 200-300 pieces. His mailing address is:

Frank H. McNamee
27 Marion Avenue
Norwood, Massachusetts

The Wicker Porch II
13 North Water Street
Nantucket Island, Massacusetts
Frank McNamee's second wicker shop is in a charming Victorian house and includes a full line of refinished wicker in white and natural finishes circa 1870 to 1930. Open in season. Call (617) 228-1052 for further information.

Wools and Wicker
Route 6A
West Barnstable, Massachusetts
This new shop (affilated with Frank McNamee of The Wicker Porch) carries quality antique wicker as well as fine woolen goods from South America.

Benton's Wicker Unlimited
Taunton, Massachusetts
(617) 823-9487

The Wicker Lady
1197 Walnut Street
Newton Highlands, Massachusetts 02161
Owners Charlotte "Charlie" Wagner and husband Steve operate a very attractive wicker specialty shop with an average 300 piece inventory. "Charlie" is a master repair person and also does professional appraisals and promotional leasing. Nothing but the best here.

Chestnut Street Antiques
1009 Chestnut Street
Newton Upper Falls,
Massachusetts 02164
Owner Greta Sones usually carries 50-75 wicker pieces in this charming specialty shop. Open every week day all year.

Wicker Unlimited
22 Skinners Path
Marblehead, Massachusetts 01945

The Wicker Works
Rt. 2A
Littleton Common
Littleton, Massachusetts 01460
Susan and Alan Silberberg run a fine antique wicker shop with 100-125 pieces on hand at all times. Expert in-house restoration is also available.

Vanworth Antiques
23 Stevens Street
Littleton, Massachusetts 01460

MINNESOTA

American Classics
4944 Xerxes South
Minneapolis, Minnesota 55410

The Wicker Shop
2190 Mashall Avenue
St. Paul, Minnesota 55104

Wicker West
174 West 7th Street
St. Paul, Minnesota 55102

MISSOURI

Mary's
9615 Manchester
Rock Hill, Missouri 63119
A mother-daughter partnership, Mary and daughter Sally have specialized in antique wicker furniture for seven years and do their own in-house restoration.

NEW JERSEY

R. & R. Antiques
79 & 81½ Anderson Street
Hackensack, New Jersey 07601
Roz Gradinger and Joan Schiffer (a charming mother and daughter team) have put their shop on the wicker map. They are both extremely knowledgeable in the field. They run a dual-operation, with one of the two shops specializing in antique wicker furniture. Usually a 200-300 piece stock, the owners take requests for hard-to-find items.

Copper Kettle Antiques
160 Monmouth St.
Red Bank, New Jersey 07701

Spirit of '76
49 North Main
Medford, New Jersey 08055

The Wicker Yard
1104 3rd Avenue
Spring Lake, New Jersey 07762
Dee and Brian Murray own and operate the finest antique wicker shop on the Jersey Shore. The shop specializes in restoration and offers a huge selection of quality wicker for sale.

Dovetail Antiques
Columbus, New Jersey
Call Pete and Susan Tanzini at (609) 298-5245 for details and shop location.

NEW YORK

The Wicker Garden
1318 Madison Avenue
New York, New York 10028
Owner Pamela Scurry is justifiably proud of her 400+ piece inventory of fine antique wicker furniture. The Wicker Garden is probably the best known wicker specialty shop in the country due to its exposure in major interior decorating magazines. She also carries an extensive line of antique children's wicker items in her second-story annex aptly named "The Wicker Garden's Baby". Both shops are a real treat for wicker collectors. Quality, rarity and a huge selection make this a top wicker shop.

Cubbyhole Antiques
145 Main Street
Nyack, New York 10960
For many years one of the top wicker shops in the country, there is usually a 300-400 piece selection at Cubbyhole. In-house repair assures the buyer that all pieces are in excellent condition.

Circa 1890
265 East 78th St.
New York, New York 10021
(212) 734-7388
Owner Merry Gilbert runs a quality antique wicker shop with over one hundred fine pieces to choose from.

Buckboard Antiques
Box 129-08
Wallkill, New York 12589
Owners Neil and Hazel Terwilliger operate a beautiful antique wicker shop and do their own in-house restoration. They can be reached at (914) 895-3050 or 895-3154 for further information and address.

Village Interiors & Antiques
207 Main Street
Port Washington, New York 11050
Owner Pearl Straus carries at least 30 pieces of quality antique wicker at all times in her interesting Long Island shop.

Inglenook Antiques
619 Hudson Street
New York, New York 10014

Round Lake Antiques
Route 9-Box 358
Round Lake, New York 12151
Owners Dottie and Ken Thompson carry large inventory of wicker dating from late 1800s to 1930s. Also specialize in in-house repairs assuring the customer of fine condition and quality.

Dottie's Antique Wicker
28 Main Street
Warrensburg, New York 12885

Pam and Bill Kelts
18 Murray Avenue
Waterford, New York 12188

Kleptomania Antiques
62 Hooker Avenue
Poughkeepsie, New York 12601

Margot Johnson, Inc.
40 West 40th Street
New York, New York 10018
Margot Johnson's beautiful wicker shop in Manhattan is a must for serious collectors. With a high-quality inventory of 75-150 pieces on hand, Margot is known as the "cherry picker of Manhattan". Some extremely rare and even museum quality pieces here and the owner really knows her wicker.

Mary Ellen Funk
P. O. Box 811
Quoque, Long Island, New York 11959

The Gazebo
660 Madison Avenue
New York, New York 10021

Town House Treasures
191 Avenue of the Americas
New York, New York 10013

Turn of the Century Antiques
Road 2
Route 17K
Montgomery, New York 12549
Rose and Walter Kurzmann have a fine selection of wicker furniture including some of the most collectible pieces available in New York State.

Yankee Peddler Antiques
519 Hudson Street
New York, New York 10014

NORTH CAROLINA

Clara's Antiques
1912 Commonwealth Avenue
Charlotte, North Carolina 28205

OHIO

Wickering Heights
401 Superior Street
Rossford, Ohio 43460
Owner Judy "The Wiz" Sikorski is one of the most knowledgeable wicker dealers in the country. Her shop is filled with fine antique wicker treasures from all over the midwest. Expert in-house restoration assures the collector that everything for sale is in excellent condition. Miniature wicker doll house furniture is a specialty.

The Wacky Wicker Workers
Mentor, Ohio 44060
(216) 255-1172

Antiques of Chester
7976 Mayfield Road
Chesterland, Ohio 44026
Owners Jim and Marian Redmond are long-time wicker dealers, collectors and restoration specialists. They both have a deep appreciation for quality antique wicker and have repaired and/or sold some of the most unique pieces in the country over the past ten years. Extensive buying trips keep their shop well-stocked. Expert in-house restoration by the owners.

Gibson-Girl Memories
625 Main Street East
Toledo, Ohio 43605
Call (419) 691-1551 (open by appointment only).

Naylor's Wicker & Antiques
220 South Main Street
Springboro, Ohio 45066

The Wicker Shop
1125 Congress Avenue
Glendale, Ohio 45246

Windows, Walls, Wicker
2203 River Road
Maumee, Ohio 43537

OREGON

Home Comfort Antiques
811 Main
Cottage Grove, Oregon 97424

RHODE ISLAND

Benton's Wicker Unlimited
Providence, Rhode Island
(401) 461-8630

TEXAS

The Old Wicker Garden
3111 Knox
Dallas, Texas 75205
Owner Julie Teicholz runs the finest wicker specialty shop in Texas. Her fine stock is obtained on buying trips across the country.

Amity Antiques
1103 West 25th
Bryan, Texas 77801

VIRGINIA

Mr. and Mrs. William D. Critzer
773 Oyster Point Road
Newport News, Virginia 23602

Slim and Wanda Wilberger
Mr. Whisker's Attic
6315 Fairview Drive
Mechanicsville, Virginia
The Wilberger's have been selling quality wicker for the past six years. Each of their 75-100 pieces is in excellent condition.

Old Town Antiques
George Spicer
Alexandria, Virginia

The Victorian Revival
7500 Idylwood Road
Falls Church, Virginia 22043
Call (703) 573-8516 for details and address.

WASHINGTON

Wicker Design Antiques
515 15th East
Seattle, Washington 98112
   Owner Alan Serebrin is probably the biggest antique wicker dealer in the Pacific northwest. He's been in the business for over six years and does his own in-house restoration. Always several hundred pieces in stock. A quality shop.

WISCONSIN

The Wickery
644 College Street
Milton, Wisconsin 53563

CARING FOR WICKER

Although the upkeep of wicker furniture is simple and need be tended to only once a year unless otherwise warranted, it's important that the collector be aware of what materials were employed in the making of their particular piece. I must first refer the reader to the photograph of materials in the section entitled "Basic Wicker Repair Techniques." These are the foremost common materials from which wicker furniture was made and the odds are high that your piece was made entirely from one or several of these materials. If your wicker is made of reed, rattan, willow or cane a simple sprinkling with a garden hose can work wonders in keeping the piece pliable whenever it seems brittle or creeks when in use. Since these materials are completely natural and have thrived in swamplands since prehistoric times, water is needed periodically to "feed" the often dried out wicker work to insure its elasticity. On the other hand, extreme caution should be used when examining these materials, for the most common error beginners make is mistaking heavily painted fiber for reed or willow and hosing it off to sometimes disastrous results. Remember, water will do more harm than good if it is applied to man-made materials such as fiber (actually a "roll" of twisted paper stiffened with glue sizing which closely resembles reed when painted).

If you're sure your wicker is made from natural materials, water (whether hosed on, combined with a mild detergent and applied with a rag or scrubbed over hard-to-get-at places in the weave with an old toothbrush) is the most efficient way to clean a piece as well as insure its future suppleness. Whether your wicker is in its natural state or painted, the above mentioned preventive measures can prolong the life of your pieces dramatically as well as add to their overall aesthetic appeal.

If you're fortunate enough to own a piece of unpainted or "natural" wicker furniture you should know that it is much harder to find (and therefore has more value) than its painted counterpart. Most serious collectors prefer natural wicker and use the cleaning methods mentoned above to keep their pieces in good condition. Futhermore, some dealers and advanced collectors clean badly soiled natural pieces by dipping a toothbrush into a well-diluted domestic bleach mixture if they plan to refinish the piece and some reeds are noticeably darker than others. This should be done with great caution and tested on the bottom or at the back of the piece first, just in case the results are not satisfactory. Remember, all natural wicker was originally either stained or coated with a clear varnish or lacquer at the factory, so it's understandable that some of these finishes need periodical maintenance. As for my own feelings on natural wicker, I contend that the best care of all is as little as absolutely necessary. If the piece creeks when in use, hose it off to feed the reeds. If the finish seems dull, a good quality mineral oil or linseed oil applied with a soft cloth is the best remedy — for it will allow the reeds to "breathe" while at the same time give the piece a more healthy appearance.

Since natural wicker is so desirable many collectors want to know if stripping wicker furniture is possible. The answer is yes and no depending on the materials used in the making of your particular piece. If you have wicker furniture made of reed, willow, rattan, cane, or any combination of these materials it can be stripped successfully (either in a chemical tank or, in a few cases, by hand) providing the stripper is familiar with wicker and knows his or her business. If your piece is made of fiber, rush or Oriental sea grass, stripping is not advised as the chemicals tend to eat away at these materials. As for reed and willow pieces, I've seen absolute wonders worked on heavily painted wicker and, on the other hand, complete disasters. To be sure, stripping wicker is a highly controversial subject among wicker experts. Some claim that it dries out the reeds and causes irreversible damage while others insist that it can actually save dry and brittle pieces that are hopelessly globbed and therefore sealed with paint. Because some wicker pieces were painted every summer (the most popular color was white, but various shades of green, brown and red were also used), I feel that severly globbed pieces actually benefit from a quick stripping. Call your local furniture stripper or antique repair person and ask if they have stripped any wicker and what the results were. Remember, if you do decide to strip your wicker it's much better to dip a painted piece into a stripper's tank quickly and get 90% of the paint off and pick away at those stubborn places with an awl or knife rather than leave the piece in the chemicals too long and cause the reeds to become fibrous.

If you have successfully stripped a painted piece of wicker, I would recommend hosing it off and letting it dry out completely in the sun or in a warm room for a few days. When the reeds are completely dried out, you can either leave the piece in its present "blonde" condition, stain the piece to your taste, or apply a coat of orange shellac. If you decide to stain the piece you should first visit your local hardware or paint dealer and ask to see either a sample display or a booklet which illustrates the anticipated results of various wood stains. Since stripped reed and cane most resembles light wood surfaces, I would use the pine samples as a point of reference. When you feel you have found the right stain, test it out first on a hidden area of the piece and wait for the results before proceeding with the entire job. If you want to darken the stain, simply apply another thin coat (allowing adequate time for drying between each application) until the desired hue is obtained. Of course, if you prefer to keep the light blonde tone of your wicker, a stain is not necessary but to bring out its original glossy appearance, I would recommend applying a light coat of orange shellac. This honey-colored shellac is made naturally by insects and the substance is passed into sheets in the Orient. Although some hunting is usually necessary to find a store that carries the product, it's one of the best protective finishes for natural wicker because it imparts a robust sheen to the reeds while not completely sealing them off from necessary moisture.

Unfortunately, white wicker or pieces which were painted to match the decor of a certain room are far more prevalent than natural wicker furniture. Regardless if those summer paintings for porch and outdoor use have chipped away or if you simply want to match your decor, if you decide to paint your wicker I would recommend contacting a professional in the field for a top quality and long-lasting paint job. Many of the people listed in the section entitled "Professional Wicker Restoration Specialists" have had a good deal of experience in painting wicker. These experts know what type of paint is best for your particular wicker piece and usually have the facilities to apply the paint with a compressor for a superior job. However, if you insist on painting your own wicker, I would recommend using a compressor and a high-grade acrylic enamel paint (either Sherwin-Williams automotive paint combined with a reducing compound or "wicker craft paint", which is a lustrous and durable gloss white enamel sold by some of the companies listed in the section entitled "Craft Supply Houses"). Whether sprayed or brushed on, oil base paints work best on wicker because of their durability, glossy sheen and resistance to "blistering" when applied over previous coats of paint. Never use Latex paint on wicker furniture.

As an added note, if you plan to paint a piece first check under the seat for a manufacturer's label. Whether paper, metal or celluloid, these labels are valuable records to save for future generations of collectors. I recommend carefully masking off or otherwise protecting these labels before painting — thus preserving a bit of history.

GUIDELINES TO BUYING WICKER

Although many a piece of antique wicker furniture is a work of art unto itself, for purely practical reasons I would suggest that you first check the framework for loose joints, overall sturdiness and general comfort before you consider buying it. Usually made of white oak or hickory, the framework of antique wicker furniture is noticeably heavier than that of reproduction wicker imported from the Far East, which usually employs bamboo, rattan or reed in the construction of the frame. Since I will shortly be discussing the difference between antique and reproduction wicker it should suffice to say here that the strength of the framework, the quality of the materials, the beauty of the design, the age, the rarity and the overall craftsmanship employed in the making of the piece in question are all of equal importance.

Once you develop a "feel" for spotting antique wicker furniture your confidence in buying it will grow. Aside from the weight of the piece, remember to consider what materials are used in the construction — for if a piece utilizes fiber or sea grass you can be 95% sure that it was made after 1900. Lastly, a familiarity with the styles represented in the following three distinct periods of wicker design is invaluable in both the selection and accurate dating of collectible wicker furniture.

COLLECTING FOR INVESTMENT

Today antique wicker has not only attracted private collectors but also those with a keen eye for investment. Gone are the days when decorators buy a few pieces to use as accents in a room. Within the past decade there has been a tremendous upsurge in the popularity of wicker furniture and many so-called "wicker nuts" have furnished entire houses with unique as well as useful wicker pieces with investment in mind.

If you're considering investing in wicker furniture I would buy only pre-1930 pieces and place the emphasis on rarity. The value of a platform rocker is higher than a standard rocker simply because there are fewer of them around. Likewise, matching sets of wicker furniture (such as a settee, armchair and rocker) are considerably harder to find and therefore command a higher price than three non-matching pieces of the same period.

Every investor in the antique wicker field should strive for pieces which combine overall quality (in design, materials and workmanship), rarity, age and condition. Each of these aspects counts heavily when entering the rarified air of collecting for investment. A note of caution here: if you find a rare piece of wicker which is obviously in need of repair I would first contact one of the professional wicker restoration specialists listed in this book in order to determine if it is repairable. Any true investment piece should be in good condition or be capable of being restored.

Of the three separate eras of wicker furniture represented in this book (Victorian, Turn-of-the-Century and 1920s) the Victorian era will always be remembered as the Golden Age of Wicker. It marked the heyday of a significant American industry which fostered a period of bold experimentation in furniture design. Futhermore, sheer age counts when buying rare wicker and since the industry was barely on its feet in 1850 it seems obvious that any pre-1900 wicker has inherent antique value and thus has that much more going for it in the way of an investment. Unique Victorian pieces such as conversation chairs (wherein a respectable Victorian couple could sit while courting and face each other without actually touching because of an armrest-divider), fancy perambulators, firescreens studded with wooden beads and "photographers chairs" (so-called because of their extensive use as props in the portrait photography studios of the day) are all wise investments.

While virtually all wicker produced between 1900 and 1917 was handmade, the new century issued in a new era in wicker design — one which rejected ornate Victorian fancywork and replaced it with the straight-lined, angular Mission style made popular by Gustav Stickley. Many of these pieces are also an excellent investment. However, in 1917 the Lloyd loom came into the scene and ushered in an era of machine-made wicker and the wicker furniture industry never really recovered from its ill-effects. With this in mind, it's wise to stay away from machine-made wicker if your goal is investment. Now regarded as structurally and aesthetically inferior to handmade wicker made of reed or willow, the Lloyd loom pieces are easy to identify by their overall tightly woven appearance and their exclusive use of fiber as the material used in construction.

Fortunately, handmade wicker was still being made during the 1920s and these are the pieces you should be looking for if you collect anything from this period. Actually, some handmade twenties wicker is now looked upon as a good find since the Lloyd loom all but monopolized the market until, by the late twenties, three quarters of all the wicker furniture in this country was being made by machine. Unique pieces such as porch swings, phonograph cabinets and lamps were usually handmade and are thus good investments.

Pinpointing the specific year of manufacture on a given piece of wicker is virtually impossible unless the date is stamped into the underside of the seat frame. While this was fairly common practice in the 1870-1880 period, today these "stamped-in" dates are rare and can be found on only a small percentage of wicker furniture.

Since authenticating the age (or even the era) of a wicker piece is important for the investor, I've included the following guidelines for dating pieces made by the Heywood-Wakefield Company and its predecessors. Any piece of wicker furniture carrying labels can be dated thusly:

Wakefield Rattan Company (1855-1897)

Heywood Brothers & Company (1868-1897)

Heywood Brothers & Wakefield Company (1897-1921)

Heywood-Wakefield Company (established in 1921)

REPRODUCTIONS: PRO AND CON

Unless you are doing business with a reputable antique wicker dealer it is not enough to simply rely on the designs presented in the following pages to determine the age of a particular piece. While the photographs from the three periods of wicker styles can clarify important points and answer some questions, the bottom line is that you should not try to determine the approximate age of a piece solely by its design. I say this because some of the designs, especially those from the Victorian era, were "adapted" (to use as polite a term as possible) to suit the growing important market in the 1960s, and are still being made today in the Far East and elsewhere. These poor quality wicker pieces became popular in the 1960s due to their attractiveness as "alternative" furniture and their affordable price tags.

At the present time only pre-1930 wicker furniture is considered collectible. Generally speaking, the older a piece is the higher its antique value — something to remember if you plan to invest in wicker. With this in mind, a serious collector should consider the following points if there is any doubt as to the true age of a given piece of wicker:

A typical basket seat so commonly damaged in poor quality reproductions.

1. How heavy is the piece? True antique wicker was made with hardwood framework as opposed to the bamboo or rattan frames used in imported reproductions.

2. What is the quality of the materials used in the construction? Whereas collectible wicker made in the United States from 1850 to 1930 made use of quality materials, inexpensive imported reproductions utilize low quality Hong Kong reeds and fibrous cane. Look at the piece. If the reed has "whiskers" or is splitting apart you can almost be certain that it's a reproduction.

3. What is used to cap the feet of the piece in question? If you come across shiny brass caps be cautious.

4. Does the piece have an abundance of "curlicues"? This curled reed fancywork (see the design employed in the back of the reproduction chair in Photo 1) is very often overdone in imported Victorian-type reproductions.

5. Does the piece have a round "basket" seat? These circular seats which employ an "under-and over" weave (see the damaged seat in Photo 1) are often the first thing to be damaged on a reproduction. Practically all old wicker made use of cane seats (either woven over or set into a hardwoood frame), horizontally woven reed seats in the under-and-over weave or springs which were originally intended for a cushion.

The best way to protect yourself against unknowingly buying a reproduction is to educate yourself. Visit antique shops that specialize in collectible wicker, and then drop in on some well-stocked import shops in order to compare the old with the new. Once you have a frame of reference it isn't hard to develop an eye for antique wicker furniture.

However, if you're consciously going out to buy a reproduction in order to fill out a collection or to add as an accent piece, there's good news concerning fine handmade wicker reproductions. In the past decade the art of bringing back quality Victorian and 1920s wicker designs has been given a second life by a handful of artisans and a few small companies. For those collectors who want to buy reproductions for one reason or another I would recommend the following three establishments:

The Hays House of Wicker
1730 East Walnut
Pasadena, California

The Hays House of Wicker stands alone in both the quality of the craftsmanship and quantity of designs readily available on the showroom floor. Owner Don Hays realizes there is a certain stigma attached to the word "reproduction" (he prefers to use the word "new"), but there is rarely an argument among experts as to the superior quality of his wicker. When his craftsmen, five very talented brothers, are given the task of purposely reproducing an original wicker design, the finished piece can be amazingly similar to its antique counterpart. Using hardwood frames, cane seats and hand-picked reeds from the nearby "Cane & Basket Supply Company" in Los Angeles, the brothers can also accurately match wicker furniture pieces. Starting out in the antique wicker and restoration field in the early 1970s, Mr. Hays found that some of the wicker repair jobs brought to his shop entailed stripping old materials down to the frame. One day it occured to him that it wouldn't be much more difficult to make the frames himself too and before long he was in the business of producing his own wicker furniture. Today his main shop in Pasadena consists of approximately one-third antique wicker and two-thirds new pieces.

While many of Mr. Hays' reproductions are sturdier than the low quality wicker sold at department stores such as Montgomery Ward around the turn-of-the-century, many wicker pursuers sniff at any new wicker just as a matter of principle. Although I can see their point that "antique value" is just as important as craftsmanship, I feel the people at the Hays House of Wicker should be recognized and given a good deal of credit for producing exceptional new wicker furniture and refusing to use inexpensive materials or machines. Indeed, Mr. Hays attaches metal labels to his wicker and it shouldn't take a visionary to realize that his fine pieces are destined to join the ranks of future wicker collectibles.

Windsor's Cane & Wicker Repair
130 East 17th Street
Suite G
Costa Mesa, California 92627

Owner-artisan Mike Bradbury is a very talented wicker restoration specialist (he began repairing in the early 1970s) who branched out into making Victorian-style to 1920s handmade wicker furniture in 1980. He runs a one-man operation, and is quite willing to duplicate existing designs or work with customers on custom pieces.

Classic Wicker
8532 Melrose Ave.
Los Angeles, CA 90069

Owner Michael Carlson carries a fine line of quality wicker reproductions based on Victorian designs. All pieces enjoy hardwood frames, cane seats and quality reeds.

Benton's Wicker Unlimited
Taunton, Massachusetts
(617) 823-9487

Roger and Patti Benton create fine wicker reproductions, including etágeres and ottomans. Custom pieces made to order.

Garnett's Wicker Shop
Route 6 Box 39
Decatur, Alabama 35603

Mrs. Garnett Drake has been making quality reproductions at affordable prices for the past three years. Her highly personalized line includes loveseats, chairs, tables, tea carts, lounges, planters and lamp shades.

BASIC WICKER REPAIR TECHNIQUES

The purpose of this section is to illustrate that some *minor* repair jobs can be accomplished by the layman if he or she is willing to purchase the correct materials and invest a little time and patience to restore a lightly damaged piece of wicker furniture. Don't try to repair anything you have doubts about . . . you just might do more harm than good. In fact, for anything more serious than the following basic step-by-step repair techniques, I would suggest contacting a professional wicker restoration specialist. These craftspeople have years of experience in this field and can work wonders on damaged wicker as well as solve difficult structural problems and accurately match existing stains on natural pieces.

MATERIALS

If you decide to tackle a simple repair job yourself you should know that collectible wicker furniture has been made from over a dozen types of materials and that two or three of these materials were often combined in the making of a single piece. However, by far the most common materials used were reed, cane, Oriental sea grass and fiber (see Photo 1). In order to determine which type of material your piece is made of, simply break off a damaged piece and compare it with the samples shown. Once you determine the type and size of materials needed, either bring your sample to a well-stocked craft supply shop or send them along to one of the craft supply houses listed in the following section in order to obtain an accurate match.

After you have purchased the needed materials you're almost ready to start repairing, but before you begin you should know that reed (both round and flat varieties) must be soaked in water for at least twenty minutes to insure flexibility and easy handling. Although cane, fiber and Oriental sea grass can be worked with ease while dry, reed *must* be soaked or it will snap.

(PHOTO 1)

From left to right: Reed, Cane, Oriental sea grass and Fiber.

TOOLS

The tools and other supplies needed for wicker repair are simple and few. A hammer; a pair of sharp hand clippers; a good quality white glue; and a supply of ½-¾ inch wire nails is all you'll need.

BASIC REPAIR METHODS

(PHOTO 2)

WRAPPING WITH CANE. By far the most common and easily solved problem with damaged wicker furniture is that the cane wrapping around a chair leg has come unraveled. The material used for this job is usually "binder cane" — a slightly wider variety of cane than which is commonly used for caning chair seats. Flat reed was also used on some pieces. After determining the correct material to use, it is always best to turn a chair over and work on it with the legs sticking up for easy access. First remove all damaged cane and nail down the end piece on the inside of the chair leg where it will not show. Then nail a new length of binder cane over the end of the old piece (Photo 2) and start wrapping the cane up the leg — being careful to wrap it tightly and evenly all the way up. When the wrapping process is completed nail off the cane about ¾ of an inch from the end of the chair leg (Photo 3) and snip the excess cane off with hand clippers. Note: for extra strength run a bead of white glue along the length of bare wood to be wrapped, thus insuring a long-lasting hold.

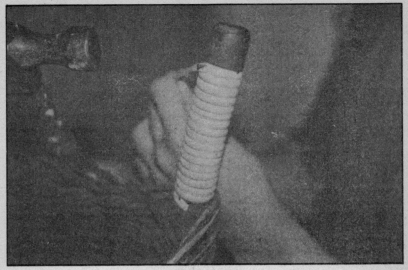

(PHOTO 3)

REPLACING "SPOKES". Replacing "spokes" (the vertical reeds over which the horizontal reeds are woven) is a fairly simple job. First the broken reed must be removed by snipping it out from the top and bottom of the second or third row of the woven horizontal reeds (Photo 4). After removing the vertical spoke replace it with a new pre-soaked length of reed (Photo 5). Remember to apply a bead of glue to each end of the new spoke to insure a tight "bond".

The only real trick to replacing spokes is in accurately duplicating the original pattern. For instance, on most pieces the spokes are slanted in one direction at the front of the chair and those at the back slant in the opposite direction. Because of this it is sometimes wise to make a sketch of the pattern before removing any reeds. The closer you can come to reproducing the existing design the better your repair job will blend in with the original wickerwork.

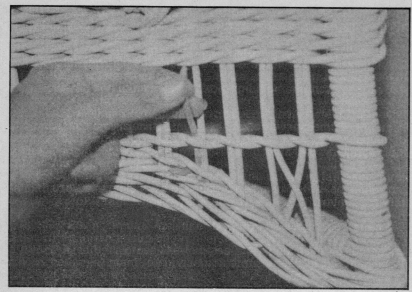

(PHOTO 4)

(PHOTO 5)

THE UNDER-AND-OVER WEAVE. If you have a wicker piece which is missing several rows in the horizontal weave but all the spokes are intact it's best to first cut away weak or uneven reeds and start fresh. Don't be afraid to cut away these damaged reeds as it is usually more time consuming to try to save them and the strength of the repair job suffers in the long run. A length of damaged horizontal reeds can be snipped out to the point where the existing weave is intact (see Photo 6) and then the worker should clip the last existing horizontal reed off behind the spoke so as to hide the cut. From this point a nes pre-cut and pre-soaked length of reed can be woven into place by using the under-and-over weave. The first row to be woven should be exact opposite of the last row left intact directly below it (see Photo 7). The technique is well-named, for the job consists of weaving under one spoke and over the next. The end result should look uniform and tight (see Photo 8). Note: For added strength place a bead of white glue where the new horizontal reed lays across each spoke.

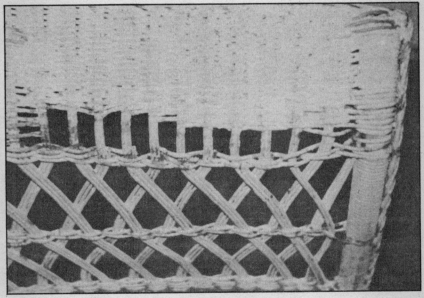

(PHOTO 6)

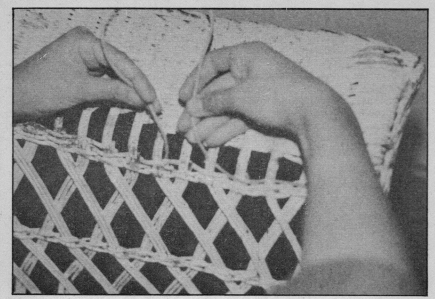

(PHOTO 7)

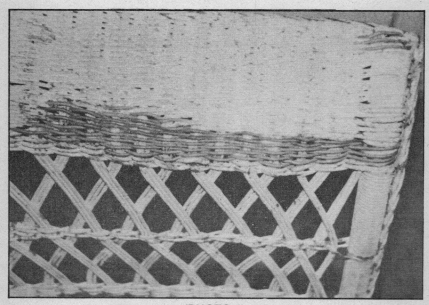

(PHOTO 8)

CRAFT SUPPLY HOUSES

If you decide to repair your own wicker furniture first check the yellow pages of your local phone book under "Arts & Crafts Supply", "Caning" and "Rattan" for businesses that carry the appropriate supplies. Unfortunately, most general craft shops carry a limited selection of wicker repair materials and very often the quality is second rate. If this is the case in your area, I would advise sending a small sample of the material you wish to duplicate to one of the following mail-order craft supply houses. The owners of these companies are usually very helpful and most will tell you what the material is, how much it will cost and how to order it through their illustrated catalogues.

ALABAMA

Garnett's Wicker Shop
Route 6, Box 39
Decatur, Alabama 35603

CALIFORNIA

Cane & Basket Supply Company
1283 South Cochran Avenue
Los Angeles, California 90019

Frank's Cane & Rush Supply
7244 Heil Avenue
Huntington Beach, California 92647

Naturalcraft Inc.
2199 Bancroft Way
Berkeley, California 94704

Nasco Handcrafters
1524 Princeton Avenue
Modesto, California 95350

T. I. E., Inc.
P.O. Box 1121
San Mateo, California 94403

The Caning Shop
926 Gilman Street at 8th
Berkeley, California 94710

COLORADO

**Greentree Ranch Wools and
 Countryside Hand-Weavers**
163 North Carter Lake Road
Loveland, Colorado 80537

Loomcraft
Box 65
Littleton, Colorado 80160

Skyloom Fibres
1905 South Pearl
Denver, Colorado 80210

CONNECTICUT

**Connecticut Cane & Reed
 Company**
P.O. Box 1276
Manchester, Connecticut 06040

The H. H. Perkins Company
10 South Bradley Road
Woodbridge, Connecticut 06525

FLORIDA

Von Wood Products
571 N. W. 71st Street
Miami, Florida 33150

ILLINOIS

Bersted's
521 West 10th Avenue
Box 40
Monmouth, Illinois 61462

Dick Blick Company
P.O. Box 1267
Galesburg, Illinois 61401

Family Weaver
1615 Crain
Evanston, Illinois
Peoria, Illinois 60202

Newell Workshop
19 Blaine Avenue
Hinsdale, Illinois 60521

Peoria Arts & Crafts Supplies
1207 Main Street
Peoria, Illinois 61607

MARYLAND

Macmillan Arts & Crafts
9645 Gerwig Lane
Columbia, Maryland 21046

MASSACHUSETTS

J. L. Hammett Company
Hammett Place
Braintree, Massachusetts 02184

The Whitaker Reed Company
90 May Street
Box 172
Worcester, Massachusetts 01602

MICHIGAN

Bexell & Son
2470 Dixie Highway
Pontiac, Michigan 48055

Traditional Handcrafters
571 Randolph Street
Northville, Michigan 48071

MINNESOTA

Maid of Scandinavia Company
3244 Raleigh Avenue
Minneapolis, Minnesota 55416

MISSOURI

WSI Distributors
1165 First Capitol Drive
P.O. Box 1235
St. Charles, Missouri 63301

NEW HAMPSHIRE

New Hampshire Cane & Reed Co.
65 Turnpike Street
Suncook, New Hampshire 03275

NEW JERSEY

Boin Arts & Crafts Company
87 Morris Street
Morristown, New Jersey 07960

Oldenbrook Spinnery Inc.
Road 1
Mountain Avenue
Lebanon, New Jersey 08833

NEW YORK

Peerless Rattan & Reed Mfg. Co.
222 Lake Avenue
P.O. Box 636
Yonkers, New York 10702

Albert Constantine & Son
2050 Eastchester Road
Bronx, New York 10461

Craftsman Supply House
35 Brown's Avenue
Scottsville, New York 14546

Eli Caning Shop
86 Wood Road
Centereach, New York 11702

The Workshop
P.O. Box 158
Pittsford, New York 14534

NORTH CAROLINA

A 'NL's Hobbycraft, Inc.
50 Broadway
P.O. Box 7025
Asheville, North Carolina 28807

Billy Arthur, Inc.
University Mall
Chapel Hill, North Carolina 27514

Earth Guild, Inc.
Hot Springs, North Carolina 28743

OHIO

Cane Shop
15635 Madison Avenue
Cleveland, Ohio 44107

Ohio Chair Company, Inc.
3447 West 130th
Cleveland, Ohio 44111

Scandinavian Art Handicraft
7696 Carmago Road
Cincinnati, Ohio 45243

Yellow Springs Strings, Inc.
Box 107
Kings Yard
Yellow Springs, Ohio 45387

OREGON

Wildflower Fibres
211 N. W. Davis Street
Portland, Oregon 97209

PENNSYLVANIA

Woodcrafter's Supply, Inc.
7703 Perry Highway-Rt. 19
Pittsburgh, Pennsylvania 15237

SOUTH CAROLINA

**Bradshaw Manufacturing
  Company**
Box 425
West Columbia, South Carolina
  29169

TENNESSEE

The Tennessee Craftsmen
5014 North Broadway
Knoxville, Tennessee 37917

UTAH

Intertwine
101 Trolley Square
Salt Lake City, Utah 84102

Zim's
P.O. Box 7620
Salt Lake City, Utah 84107

WASHINGTON

Northwest Cane Supply
8010 15th N. W.
Seattle, Washington 98117

Northwest Looms
Box 10369
Brainbridge Island, Washington
  98110

WISCONSIN

Bluemound Crafts
Box 1579
1000 North Bluemound Road
Appleton, Wisconsin 54911

Nasco Handcrafters
901 Janesville Avenue
Fort Atkinson, Wisconsin 53538

Sax Arts & Crafts
316 North Milwaukee Street
P.O. Box 2002
Milwaukee, Wisconsin 53538

The Handcrafters
1 West Brown Street
Waupun, Wisconsin 53963

CANADIAN
CRAFT SUPPLY HOUSES

Handcraft Woods
Box 378
Streetsville, Ontario
Canada

Leclerc Weaving Center
9210 Lajeunesse Street
Montral, H2M 1S2
Canada

PROFESSIONAL WICKER RESTORATION SPECIALISTS

Since many professional wicker repair people rely on word-of-mouth advertising, I must caution the reader that the following list is by no means a comprehensive survey of the artisans now active in this highly specialized field. While I have done my best to include wicker repair people that I have known and corresponded with over the past eight years (as well as devouring hundreds of telephone books for possible listings) it's virtually impossible to compile a complete list. With this in mind the owner of a piece of wicker in need of repair should not despair if a local wicker repair person is not included in the following list. Use your ingenuity by thumbing through your local yellow pages and looking under the following headings:

Antiques
Antiques — Repair and Restoration
Furniture — Repairing and Refinishing
Caning
Rattan
Reed

You can also do a little detective work of your own by calling the owners of these businesses and simply ask them if they know of anyone who repairs wicker furniture. If nothing turns up here you might want to call local craft shops for possible repair people who have left their business cards. Remember, some wicker repair people can be fine craftsmen and craftswomen who simply work out of their home to supplement their incomes and do not make enough money from repair jobs to justify investing in an ad in the yellow pages.

Qualified wicker restoration specialists (whether they own their own wicker specialty shops or work out of their homes) are a breed apart. These craftspeople have a deep appreciation for antique wicker and have a genuine "feel" for each piece in regards to bringing it back to its original condition. While many buy up damaged wicker and restore it to sell to wicker specialty shops, still others insist on repairing pieces for the public only. Of course, the majority of these specialists repair for shops as well as the public but be advised that some of these craftspeople differ in their attitudes as to what is worth restoring. For instance, some "purists" refuse to repair the machine-made wicker furniture from the twenties made of fiber. In any case, these uniquely talented people can perform near miracles on damaged wicker that would have been thrown away without a second thought a mere decade ago (see Photos before you head for the dump!).

Whether it's a structural problem, an extensive reweaving job or the meticulous matter of matching the original stain on a repaired section, the truly qualified wicker specialist is a virtual gold mine to the collector and can enhance the beauty and value of collectible wicker many times over.

If and when you do manage to locate a wicker restoration specialist I would recommend that you ask to see either a wicker piece they are presently restoring or a photographic record of a "before and after" repair job. If the repair person has no proof of his or her ability I would be

Before

After one-half of the repairs have been completed.

leary of their expertise. I say this because the great majority of professional wicker restoration specialists approach their work as a matter of pride in rediscovering and mastering what was thought to be a "lost art" only a few years ago.

Again, I've taken the liberty of adding comments under the names of those wicker restoration specialists whom I have had the pleasure of meeting or corresponding with over the past five years. However, these comments in no way lessen the abilities of those wicker repair people who are included in this list yet have no comment attached to their names or shops.

ALABAMA

Allen's Antiques & Collectibles
121 Telegraph Road
Chickasaw, Alabama 36610
Pat and Frank Allen have been doing fine wicker restoration work in the Mobile area for the past six years.

Mrs. Garnett Drake
Garnett's Wicker Shop
Route 6, Box 39
Decatur, Alabama 35603
Mrs. Drake is one of the top wicker repair specialists in the south. She has many years of experience in wicker restoration and also creates quality reproduction pieces on order.

ARIZONA

The Seat Weaving Shop
2214 North 24th Street
Phoenix, Arizona 85024
Owner Lynn Cook and her partners have been restoring antique wicker for several years and do expert work.

In Days of Old
2217 North 7th Street
Phoenix, Arizona 85024

ARKANSAS

Charlotte Thompson
1544 Crestwood
North Little Rock, Arkansas 72116

CALIFORNIA

The Hays House of Wicker
1730 East Walnut
Pasadena, California 91106
Owner Don Hays has in his employ five extremely talented brothers who can work miracles with wicker. Not only are they restoration specialists, the brothers also make the best quality new wicker furniture in the country.

Mike Bradbury
Windsor's Cane & Wicker
 Repair
130 East 17th Street
Suite G
Costa Mesa, California 92627
A master repairman, owner Mike Bradbury began restoring antique wicker in the early 1970's and is now one of the country's top experts. He also began making quality new wicker furniture in 1980.

Lightfoot House
8259 Melrose Avenue
Los Angeles, California 90046
Dale Beebe has been restoring antique wicker out of his shop for some 17 years. Top-quality workmanship.

Dr. Peter J. Isgrow
Isgrow & Company
1125 Soquel Avenue
Santa Cruz, California 95062
The good doctor is a talented repairman and has also developed a highly effective method of hand-stripping heavily varnished wicker and refinishing it to its original condition.

AAA-1 Jim & Sons
775 Filbert
San Francisco, California 94133

Agelong
1102 Hyde
San Francisco, California 94109

Alex Rattan-Wicker-Cane Shop
123 South San Gabriel
San Gabriel, California 91776

Cane & Basket Supply Company
1283 South Cochran Avenue
Los Angeles, California 90019

Colonial Crafters
1943 Franfort Street
San Diego, California 92110

Lew Tut
2615 South El Camino Real
San Mateo, California 94401

Kurt L. Skelton
Tanglewood Furniture Restoration
325 Pennsylvania Avenue
Santa Cruz, California 95062
Owner Kurt Skelton has been restoring wicker for eight years and is one of the top repairmen in California. Complete structural work, expert caning and refinishing also available.

The Caning Place
2611 Calhoun
Alameda, California 94501

The Caning Shop
926 Gilman
Berkeley, California 94710
Owner Jim Widess runs an excellent repair shop with several expert repair people in his employ. Mr. Widess has also written the most comprehensive book on caning I've ever seen. The Caner's Handbook can be ordered directly from his shop in Berkeley or from Van Nostrand Reinhold in New York.

The Finishing Touch
5636 College Avenue
Oakland, California 94618

The Wicker Warehouse
506 West 1st Street
Claremont, California 91711

The Wicker Warehouse
965 West 2nd
Pomona, California 91766

CONNECTICUT

Henry Spieske
The Wicker Fixer
(Connecticut Antique Wicker)
1052 Rear Main Street
Newington, Connecticut 06111
Master craftsman Henry Spieske takes his wicker restoration work seriously. With customers as far away as Florida, he has developed a good reputation in the field over the past several years. After seeing "before-and-after" repair photos of a wicker china closet caught in a fire, I can personally vouch for his expertise. Henry is considered by many experts to be the top wicker restoration specialist in the country.

John P. Gerbasi
Priscilla Furniture, Inc.
355 Post Road
Darien, Connecticut 06820

Dick Alexander
Yesterday's Yankee
Lovers Lane
Lakeville, Connecticut 06039

Paul's Furniture Repair Shop
23 First Street
East Norwalk, Connecticut 06855

FLORIDA

Frantiques Antique Wicker
1109½ West Water Avenue
Tampa, Florida 33604

Antiques & Wicker Sales
1425 W. Busch Boulevard
Tampa, Florida 33612

Dennis Beaver
The Key West Wicker Works
913 Duval Street
Key West, Florida 33040
Dennis Beaver not only does fine wicker repair but he is also the owner of the "Wickerhouse" — a wicker-filled inn located at the same address.

Kathy Bondhus
Antique Wicker
5150 S.W. 60th Place
Miami, Florida 33155
   Owner Kathy Bondhus specializes in wicker refinishing and lacquering aside from being an experienced wicker repair person.

Michael Calyore
5307 Shirley Street
Naples, Florida 33942

Den of Antiquity
831-B N. Federal Highway
Ft. Lauderdale, Florida 33304
   Owners Bud Markwell and Richard Daniel do fine wicker restoration as well as caning, rushing and splinting.

Von Wood Products
571 N. W. 71st Street
Miami, Florida 33311

GEORGIA

W. B. Lewis
231 Chatham Avenue
Pooler, Georgia 31322
   A very talented wicker repairman, Mr. Lewis receives pieces from all over the country and recommends that travelers on the east coast on their way to Florida arrange to leave pieces for repair to be picked up on their return.

Sheralyn's Antiques
1056 Murphy Avenue
Atlanta, Georgia 30310

HAWAII

Choi's Wicker Furniture Shop
260 Kilauea Avenue
Oahu, Hawaii 96816

**L. C. S. Custom Furniture &
   Refinishing**
891 Alua Street
Bay 7 Wailuku, Maui
Hawaii 96793

ILLINOIS

Bill and Lee Stewart
The Collected Works
905 Ridge Road
Willmette, Illinois 60091
   A highly-talented husband and wife team, the Stewarts have been restoring antique wicker since the early 1970's and all of their work is guaranteed. True experts in the field, they are a valuable resource to any serious collector.

Kathy Olin
Route 1
Mt. Vernon, Illinois 62864
   A talented repair person, Mrs. Olin has restored antique wicker furniture for several years and has taught wicker repair at Southern Illinois University in Carbondale.

Alex Fitch Furniture Restoration
1227 West Altgeld
Chicago, Illinois 60614

Ed Ganshirt
810 Park Avenue
Galena, Illinois 61036

INDIANA

Vic and Anne Durkin
Antique Repair Shoppe
7222 Magoun Avenue
Hammond, Indiana 46324
   The Durkins have been doing excellent repair work for several years.

Mary Kihlstrum
Scrounger's Delight
1102 Esplanade
Lafayette, Indiana 47905

Ron Rouser
The Yellow Wagon
400 West Melbourne
Logansport, Indiana 46947

Tom Duncan
P.O. Box 481
Syracuse, Indiana 46567
Mr. Duncan is an excellent repairman and has also written a fine guide on wicker himself. **How To Buy and Restore Wicker Furniture** *is available from his own publishing company at the above address.*

IOWA

Kathy Glasgow
R. R. 1
Box 162
Danville, Iowa 52623
A well-qualified wicker restoration specialist, Mrs. Glasgow also does hand caning and rush seating.

Beldings Furniture Restoration
2734 Mt. Vernon Road S. E.
Cedar Rapids, Iowa 52403

Wilson's Wicker & Weaving
1509 Main Street
Cedar Falls, Iowa 50613

LOUISIANA

The Wicker Gazebo
3137 Magazine Street
New Orleans, Louisiana 70115

MAINE

Elizabeth and Richard King
Antique Wicker
Main Street
Northeast Harbor, Maine 04662
Longtime wicker restoration specialists, the Kings have their beautiful wicker specialty shop here and do excellent work.

MARYLAND

Linda and Gary Koch
The Wicker Lady of Maryland
505 Jumpers Hole Road
Severna Park, Maryland 21146

Margaret Whippee
Whippee's Wicker
523 Herring Avenue
Fairhaven, Maryland 20754

Len's Country Barn Antiques
9929 Rhode Island Avenue
College Park, Maryland 20740

MASSACHUSETTS

Frank H. McNamee
The Wicker Porch
Route 28
Cranberry Highway
Wareham, Massachusetts 02571
One of the best wicker repairmen in the country, Mr. McNamee is carrying on in the tradition of fine New England craftsmen that have come before him. Mailing address:

Frank H. McNamee
27 Marion Avenue
Norwood, Massachusetts 02062

Benton's Wicker Unlimited
Taunton, Massachusetts
(617) 823-9487
Roger and Patti Benton have been restoring antique wicker for the past decade. They excell in all phases of repair.

Charlotte Wagner
The Wicker Lady
1197 Walnut Street
Newton Highlands, Massachusetts 02161
"Charlie" Wagner and husband Steve have been restoring antique wicker for several years and do top-quality work.

Bostonia Furniture Company
183 Friend Street
Boston, Massachusetts 02114

Jack L. Blake
7 Dr. Lord's Road
Dennis, Massachusetts 02638

Van Worth Antiques
23 Stevens Street
Littleton, Massachusetts 01460

Marla Segal
Wicker Unlimited
22 Skinners Path
Marblehead, Massachusetts 01945

MICHIGAN

Nancy Stanley
Hale, Michigan 48739
(517) 537-4874 or 728-2584

Lois's Enterprises
2444 24 Mile
Rochester, Michigan
(313) 748-3859 Summer
(313) 739-7721
    Lois specializes in chair caning, rushing and wicker repair.

MINNESOTA

Theodore and Elaine Kvasnik
The Wicker Shop
2040 Marshall Avenue
St. Paul, Minnesota 55104

The Wicker Shop
2190 Marshall Avenue
St. Paul, Minnesota 55104

Wicker West Repair Shop
174 West 7th Street
St. Paul, Minnesota 55410

MISSOURI

Cheri and Mike Russell
The Wicker Fixer
Route 1 Box 283-B
Ozark, Missouri 65721
    Cheri and Mike Russell have been repairing wicker for several years and also strip and refinish antique wicker to perfection.

Mary's
9615 Manchester
Rock Hill, Missouri 63119

NEW JERSEY

Dee and Brian Murphy
The Wicker Yard
1104 3rd Avenue
Spring Lake, New Jersey 07762

Marcey Hedgepeth
Route 179
Ringoes, New Jersey 08551

Jones Antiques
Oak Road & Harding Highway
Buena Acres, New Jersey

NEW YORK

Hazel & Neil Terwilliger
Buckboard Antiques
Box 129-08
Wallkill, New York 12589
    A talented husband and wife repair team with several years experience. Call (914) 895-3796 or 895-3154 for further information and address.

Pam Thompson
Wacky Wicker Worker II
P.O. Box 1
Constantia, New York 13044
    Mrs. Thompson is a talented second-generation wicker repair specialist. Her parents Jim and Marian Redmond (the Wacky Wicker Workers of Ohio) are rightly proud of her accomplishments.

Bressler Chair Caning Company
1268 Saint Nicholas Avenue
(17th Street)
New York, New York 10033

Tony Karlovich
Cubbyhole Antiques
145 Main Street
Nyack, New York 10960

Dottie and Ken Thompson
Round Lake Antiques
Route 9, Box 358
Round Lake, New York 12151

Pat Steinbeiser
The Wicker Witch Shop
6 Bradley Street
Marcellus, New York 13108

NORTH CAROLINA

Clara H. Gault
Clara's Antiques
1912 Commonwealth Ave.
Charlotte, North Carolina 28205

OHIO

Judy Sikorski
The Wicker Wizard
401 Superior Street
Rossford, Ohio
 Judy "The Wiz" Sikorski is one of the most gifted wicker repair people in the country. This energetic dynamo not only repairs and sells antique wicker but also teaches a university course on the subject. Husband Jim also helps in the repair process and is an experienced woodworker. Extra attention is given to all wicker being restored, although The Wiz specializes in Victorian pieces.

Jim and Marian Redmond
Wacky Wicker Workers
Mentor, Ohio 44060
 The Redmond's are an extremely talented husband and wife restoration team. Jim has developed a vise-like "curlicue machine" to help cut down the time usually required to make these fancywork designs. Marian specializes in making beautiful wicker lampshades (woven over sturdy wooden frames made by Jim) and has a sixth sense when it comes to creating a shade that compliments an existing lamp base. Call them at (216) 255-1172 for further information and address.

Howard Secrest
2976 Bishop
Cleveland, Ohio 44143

Ohio Chair Company, Inc.
3447 West 130th Street
Cleveland, Ohio 44111

Kim Terlecky
The Wicker Picker
530 East Philadelphia Ave.
Youngstown, Ohio 44502

Edward Roughton
The Wicker Shop
2011 Cleveland Road
Sandusky, Ohio 44870

OKLAHOMA

Loren L. Lewis, Jr.
1228 North Yale
Tulsa, Oklahoma 74115
 An all-around craftsman, Mr. Lewis has successfully repaired antique wicker furniture for several years.

Nelson's Furniture Refinishing &
 Repair
1112 North Broadway
Oklahoma City, Oklahoma 73103

OREGON

Sue Kaady
14915 South Greentree Drive
Oregon City, Oregon 97045
 Sue Kaady is a master repair person with several years experience in the antique wicker field. She also makes some of the finest custom wicker miniatures in the entire country and is capable of producing a tiny "clone" of your favorite wicker piece.

Donna Allison
The Wicker Workshop
115 West California Street
P.O. Box 584
Jacksonville, Oregon 97530

Bob Bennett's 13th Avenue
 Stripper
8225 S. E. 13th
Portland, Oregon 97202

Royce and Donna Hardester
The Wicker Fixer
707 Jackson
Oregon City, Oregon 97045

Kathleen Lynch Caning, Rush &
 Wicker Repair
87867 Cedar Flat Road
Springfield, Oregon 97477

PENNSYLVANIA

Carolyn Volk
240 Neely School Road
Wexford, Pennsylvania 15090

RHODE ISLAND

Benton's Wicker Unlimited
Providence, Rhode Island
(401) 461-8630

TENNESSEE

Jack and Julia Jennings
Wicker King
8241 Highway 70 South
Nashville, Tennessee 37221

TEXAS

Julie Teicholz
The Old Wicker Garden
3111 Knox
Dallas, Texas 75205

Jane Davis
The Gibson Girl
2644 W. 34th
Amarillo, Texas 79109
A multi-talented woman, Ms. Davis has been a wicker restoration specialist for several years and is also a gifted interior decorator.

Amity Antiques
1103 West 25th
Bryan, Texas 77801

The Chair Repair Company
5807 Star
Houston, Texas 77057

The Cunningham Crew
131 South Lancaster
Dallas, Texas 75203

The Wicker Doctor
327 Summertime
San Antonia, Texas 78216

Robert and Patricia Morgan
Antique Wicker and Wood Restoration
104 South Tumbleweed Trail
Austin, Texas 78746

VIRGINIA

Mr. and Mrs. William D. Critzer
773 Oyster Point Road
Newport News, Virginia 23602

Slim and Wanda Wilberger
Mr. Whisker's Attic
6315 Fairview Drive
Mechanicsville, Virginia

The Victorian Revival
7500 Idylwood Road
Falls Church, Virginia 22043

WASHINGTON

Alan Serebrin
Wicker Design Antiques
515 15th East
Seattle, Washington 98112
A master craftsman, Mr. Serebrin has been restoring antique wicker for the past six years.

WISCONSIN

Bea Niles
The Wickery
644 College Street
Milton, Wisconsin 53563

GLOSSARY

ARABESQUES. A very intricate wickerwork pattern which interlaces flowers and other flowing designs. Strictly for ornamentation and most often found in Victorian wicker.

BAR HARBOR DESIGN. A name given to open-weave willow and reed pieces which became popular in the early 1900s, and made use of open latticework to lessen the cost of hand labor.

BINDER CANE. Cane which is slightly wider and thicker than the normal chair-seating variety. Most often used as a structural wrap on wicker furniture. Usually sold in 25 foot rolls or 500 foot "hanks".

BIRDCAGE DESIGN. A typically Victorian wicker design which (because of its unique arrangement of bowed vertical reeds) seemed to "cage" a cane-wrapped leg or back brace.

BRAIDING. A term used for a long section of reeds or fiber which have been braided together in the traditional 3-way style. Braiding was very common in 1920s wicker because it was used to finish off the rough edges where the weave ended.

CANE. The outer bark of the rattan palm which is sliced off in long thin strips. This resilient, glossy material became popular in Europe during the seventeenth century, when it was woven into the seats and backs of Flemish-style chairs.

CANE WEBBING. Sometimes called "sheet cane", this machine-made webbing is woven from natural cane and used for set-in cane seating.

CAPE COD DESIGN. Closely woven reed pieces of the early 1900s.

COMFORT ROCKER. A particularily form-fitting and popular wicker rocking chair design used from 1880 to 1910.

CURLICUE. A circular, coil-like design employed in many Victorian and early 1900 wicker pieces. Made of reed.

DIAPER PATTERN. A crisscross design that creates a diamond effect.

ELLIPTIC SPRINGS. Heavy duty ellipse-shaped metal springs usually found on Victorian platform rockers and baby carriages.

FIBER. Sometimes spelled "fibre" and sometimes called "art fibre", "fibre-rush" and "fibre-reed" in the past, this man-made (and chemically treated) twisted paper was made to resemble real twisted bull rushes. This was the material Marshall B. Lloyd put to use so effectively in the making of "Lloyd loom" furniture for the Heywood-Wakefield Company during the 1920s. (Note: at stress points in the design the fiber was often wrapped around wire to insure sturdiness and durability).

GESSOED ROSES. Moulded fancywork made from Plaster of Paris which often utilized flower wreath designs and is usually found on wicker made after 1895.

HAND-CANED SEAT. Any caned seat woven by hand rather than machine. On hand-caned seating the holes in the bottom of the seat should be clearly visible.

LOCKING. The laying together of both ends of a weaving strand.

MISSION STYLE. A style in furniture design which appeared on the scene around 1900 and described straight-lined, practical furniture. Actually an over-reaction against late Victorian excesses, the Mission style had its champion in Gustav Stickley and his "Craftsman" furniture of the early 1900s was a strong influence in simplifying elaborate wicker designs.

NATURAL WICKER. Any wicker piece left unpainted.

ORIENTAL SEA GRASS. A natural, twine material twisted to resemble rope. Made of a natural straw-like product which is varigated green and tan in color. Sea grass is hand twisted and therefore the thickness may vary slightly within a coil (approximately three pounds).

OSIERS. Supple twigs from willow trees which are peeled and soaked to insure flexibility in the making of willow furniture.

PHOTOGRAPHER'S CHAIR. Sometimes called "posing chairs" or "Fancy Reception Chairs", these extremely ornate pieces were used in Victorian and turn-of-the-century portrait photography studios.

PLATFORM ROCKERS. Wicker platform rockers were designed to prevent rug wear and were attached by powerful metal springs (usually coil or elliptic) to a stationary "platform" base.

PRAIRIE GRASS. A natural, twisted straw material used in many 1910-1930 wicker pieces. It closely resembles Oriental sea grass.

RAFFIA. A course fiber cut from the leafstalks of the raphia palm in Madagascar and sometimes used in the wrapping or fancywork of post-Victorian wicker furniture.

RATTAN. A climbing palm native to the East Indies which, by means of stout reversed thorns on its leaves, winds its way up neighboring trees and can attain lengths of up to six hundred feet without exceeding an inch and a half in diameter. It is from the rattan palm that we obtain cane (its outer coating) and reed (its inner pith).

REED. The extraordinary pliable inner-pith of the rattan palm. First used in the 1850s, reed is the most common of materials used in the construction of collectible wicker furniture. Use in both round and flat varieties.

ROSETTES. A circular rose-like design most often decorating the arm tips of Victorian chairs and rockers.

RUSH. A natural, grass-like leafless stem derived from the sedge family. A perennial plant, rush was sometimes used in the making of mats, chair seats and backs.

SCROLLWORK. A flowing series of curlicues and/or fancywork which resembles breaking waves.

SEA GRASS. See "Oriental Sea Grass".

SERPENTINE DESIGN. A hollow, rolled-edge technique employed in many Victorian and early 1900 wicker pieces to finish off edges and soften harsh angles.

SET-IN CANE SEAT. This technique of caning was invented by Gardner A. Watkins, an employee of Heywood Brothers and Company. Sometimes called "pre-woven" cane seats, the sheet cane webbing was made on a loom. An automatic channeling machine cut out a small groove around the wooden seat frame to allow the webbing to be attached to the shallow channel by means of a triangular-shaped reed called "spline".

SPOKES. The vertical reeds over which wickerwork is woven.

STRAPWORK. A variation of latticework.

WICKER. A cover-all term (coming into use around 1900) which describes all woven furniture made with such materials as rattan, reed, cane, willow, fiber, sea grass, rush, raffia, and numerous dried grasses.

WILLOW. These highly flexible twigs are blonde colored in their natural state and often exhibit small "knots" where tiny offshoots were removed. Since willow resembles reed, the two materials are almost indistinguishable when painted.

Recommended Reading . . .

The Official Price Guide to Wicker *is designed for the novice as well as the seasoned collector. Information on price trends, industry development, investing, and collecting techniques such as care and repair, storage, or building a collection is written in a way a beginning hobbyist will understand yet gives specific details and helpful hints the hard-core collector will find useful.*

This guide also offers up-to-date prices for both rare and common collectibles that are available in the current secondary market. This guide will give any collector confidence when determining what articles to purchase at what price. With the knowledge gained from this guide, a collector will move from flea market to auction house with ease knowing which items are "hot" and which articles are definitely overpriced.

As your interest in collecting grows, you may want to start a reference library of your favorite areas. For the collector who needs more extensive coverage of the collectibles market, The House of Collectibles publishes a complete line of comprehensive companion guides which are itemized at the back of this book. They contain full coverage on buying, selling, and caring of valuable articles, plus listings with thousands of prices for rare, unusual, and common antiques and collectibles.

$9.95-6th Edition, 1012 pp., Order #271-X

The House of Collectibles recommends *The Official Price Guide to Antiques and Other Collectibles,* sixth edition, as the companion to this guide.

- *110,000 current market values* and detailed listings represent *over 10,000 types of collectibles* from the most popular fields of collecting.

- **ACTUAL PRICES FROM THE EXPERTS** — Information is provided by a special board of collectibles experts, auction houses and specialized dealers located throughout the U.S. and Canada. These facts are compiled and analyzed by a special computerized process to provide the most accurate information available.

- **MARKET REVIEW** — Analyze this revealing discussion on last year's most popular collectibles and take advantage of valuable insight into buying and investment trends.

- **HISTORICAL NOTES AND DEFINITIONS** — Each collectible category is defined and accurate background information is included, giving the reader a basic introduction to an overwhelming array of antiques from Advertising through World's Fair collectibles.

Available from your local dealer or order direct from:
THE HOUSE OF COLLECTIBLES, see order blank

Catalogue courtesy of Mary Jean McLaughlin of "A Summer Place" in Guilford, Connecticut.

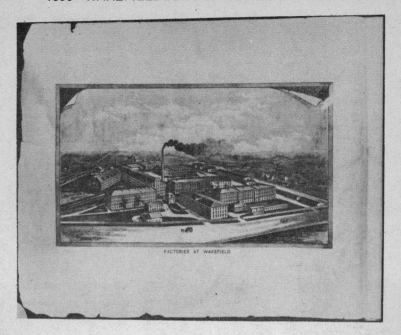

FACTORIES AT WAKEFIELD

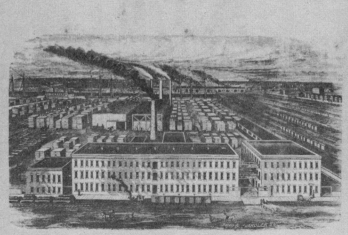

FACTORIES AT CHICAGO.

329
$125-$200

129
$125-$200

130
$150-$225

1309
$125-$200

1329
$125-$200

219
$200-$285

For the convenience of our readers, the current value range for each wicker piece appears beneath the original catalogue number.

3032
$135-$225

3033
$145-$230

3034S
$225-$300

3029
$145-$230

3030
$145-$230

3031
$200-$275

1664
$185-$285

1666S
$225-$335

1678
$200-$300

1692
$185-$285

1694S
$225-$345

1676
$175-$250

1660
$225-$325

1662S
$245-$365

1672
$200-$300

1652
$225-$325

1654S
$235-$350

1674
$225-$325

1696
$200-$300

1700
$200-$300

1656
$200-$300

1698S
$250-$350

1702S
$250-$350

1658S
$225-$325

3097
$250-$350

3098S
$300-$425

3099
$285-385

3116
$200-$300

3117S
$250-$365

3028
$185-$250

3025
$175-$250

3026
$200-$275

3027
$200-$300

1076
$200-$300

1077
$200-$300

1078
$275-$365

996
$185-$285

997
$195-$275

998
$225-$325

977
$200-$300

978
$250-$350

1327
$225-$325

1670
$225-$325

1668
$200-$300

576
$125-$165

3015
$245-$325

1446
$375-$500

3013
$300-$400

1699
$150-$250

1701
$250-$350

1705
$250-$350

484
$200-$285

1495
$200-$275

3128
$200-$300

3044
$200-$285

3005
$200-$285

3008
$225-$350

3003
$195-$250

3004
$200-$300

3045
$225-$325

3048
$200-$275

3049
$200-$300

3046
$185-$235

3014
$200-$275

3129
$200-$300

3047
$225-$335

1437
$250-$375

3007
$200-$300

3006
$225-$325

3002
$275-$375

3000
$225-$325

3130
$230-$350

1552
$200-$285

1415
$190-$250

3012
$200-$275

1554
$235-$325

1416
$240-$350

3017
$235-$350

3111
$225-$300

1120
$200-$300

485
$250-$325

3112
$225-$325

985
$250-$350

999
$250-$350

1540
$200-$300

1644
$275-$385

1695
$225-$300

1542
$200-$325

1646
$300-$450

731
$250-$340

1704
$275-$375

1706
$250-$350

1712
$275-$350

724
$235-$300

729
$250-$350

1714
$285-$375

1581
$250-$350

1716
$250-$350

1719
$250-$350

1583
$275-$375

1718
$275-$375

1720
$275-$375

1595
$250-$350

1597
$250-$350

1599
$250-$350

1708
$275-$375

1710
$260-$350

791
$250-$350

1579
$285-$385

1252
$250-$350

1365
$300-$400

1246
$235-$345

1551
$250-$350

1553
$250-$350

1613
$235-$335

1395
$235-$335

1122
$275-$375

1615
$250-$350

1396
$250-$350

1611
$300-$400

1492
$425-$550

931
$250-$350

1458
$250-$350

1493
$475-$625

933
$275-$375

1459
$275-$375

1557
$250-$340

1607
$250-$350

1453
$260-$365

1559
$260-$375

1609
$275-$385

1507
$285-$395

1144
$350-$475

1145
$375-$475

1146
$350-$450

44
$300-$375

753
$350-$450

3010
$275-$375

1502
$200-$300

3120
$300-$400

1504
$200-$300

3024
$225-$325

3121
$325-$425

1336
$375-$385

3093
$275-$375

3095
$275-$375

3118
$250-$350

3094
$300-$400

3096
$300-$400

3119
$275-$365

1422
$250-$325

1428
$250-$325

1469
$250-$320

1423
$265-$350

1425
$265-$350

1470
$265-$350

3035
$250-$325

3037
$250-$350

3039
$300-$400

3036
$300-$425

3038
$300-$425

3040
$350-$475

3124
$250-$350

3125
$275-$375

3011
$385-$475

1424
$225-$325

3016
$285-$385

1124
$400-$500

3151
$300-$400

3107
$450-$600

3001
$275-$375

3152
$325-$450

3108
$500-$650

3009
$325-$450

1429
$350-$450

3109
$375-$475

1671
$375-$475

1430
$375-$500

3110
$400-$525

1673
$400-$525

3126
$400-$500

3127
$275-$385

3164
$350-$450

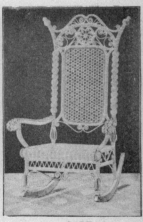

3165
$400-$550

3166
$450-$575

3167
$450-$575

3068
$300-$400

3080
$265-$350

3066
$350-$450

3069
$325-$450

3081
$300-$400

3067
$375-$485

1665
$275-$375

1272
$300-$400

1651
$375-$500

1667
$300-$400

1273
$325-$425

1653
$425-$550

1280
$300-$385

1282
$300-$425

1284
$300-$425

1281
$375-$475

1283
$400-$500

1285
$400-$500

1618
$325-$425

3041
$400-$500

3042
$350-$450

869
$325-$425

808
$350-$450

3043
$375-$485

1036
$300-$400

1037
$375-$475

940
$400-$500

806
$325-$425

1129
$300-$400

1130
$300-$400

1624
$275-$375

1432
$285-$375

1317
$225-$300

1626
$300-$425

1628
$300-$425

1318
$250-$350

1441
$300-$400

1442
$285-$400

3122
$285-$375

1443
$325-$450

1445
$325-$450

3123
$300-$400

1639
$300-$400

1641
$325-$425

1643
$350-$450

1645
$350-$450

1647
$375-$475

1649
$400-$525

1546
$275-$375

1711
$750-$1,000

1434
$250-$325

1657
$300-$425

1655
$285-$385

3104
$400-$600

3100
$285-$385

3101
$475-$575

3105
$550-$700

3102
$425-$525

3103
$650-$800

3106
$1,000-$1,350

3133
$200-$285

3132
$650-$825

3134
$250-$325

3135
$275-$375

3158
$300-$400

3131
$300-$400

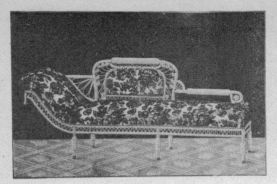

3149
$750-$1,000

3150
$200-$275

3146
$500-$650

3147
$700-$875

3148
$250-$350

3020
$285-$385

3023
$650-$800

3021
$450-$600

3019
$350-$475

3022
$750-$1,000

3018
$300-$400

3060
$275-$375

3065
$500-$675

3062
$425-$575

3061
$325-$425

3064
$750-$950

3063
$600-$750

3137
$425-$550

3139
$850-$1,200

3138
$350-$450

3136
$375-$500

3157
$300-$400

3140
$675-$800

3142
$300-$400

3143
$700-$900

3163
$750-$1,000

3141
$350-$475

3144
$600-$725

3162
$600-$850

3084
$450-$550

3086
$600-$700

1304
$600-$700

3085
$500-$650

3087
$650-$750

1305
$625-$725

866
$585-$700

3145
$1,750 +

1289
$600-$725

3170
$250-$350

3169
$500-$700

3168
$225-$300

1538
$375-$475

3050
$175-$225

1126
$500-$650

966
$500-$600

1414
$500-$625

1342
$550-$675

1604
$700-$900

829
$300-$400

1578
$135-$200

1580
$135-$200

1582
$100-$165

1564
$150-$200

1688
$175-$225

3056
$225-$325

1142
$125-$175

1143
$135-$185

1572
$125-$175

1574
$125-$175

1570
$135-$185

243
$75-$100

3077
$175-$225

3078
$185-$240

3089
$175-$235

3079
$200-$285

3074
$275-$375

3075
$285-$385

85
$175-$235

818
$175-$235

190
$195-$250

3076
$250-$325

3072
$225-$325

3073
$285-$385

1562
$175-$235

1391
$175-$260

1560
$170-$235

1558
$170-$225

1392
$225-$325

3153
$170-$245

3154
$250-$350

1393
$185-$275

3155
$375-$475

876
$250-$350

877
$285-$385

3156
$400-$525

230
$250-$350

3059
$400-$500

3058
$425-$525

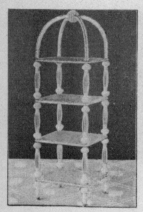

3057
$650-$850

3159
$500-$700

3160
$575-$800

3090
$250-$350

3070
$500-$750

123
$200-$300

1169
$800-$1,000

3051
$700-$900

3052
$1,100-$1,400

3053
$825-$950

1038
$700-$900

1648
$900-$1,250

1650
$1,000-$1,400

1635
$1,100-$1,400

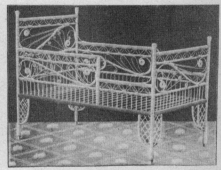

1633
$1,250-$1,500

1109
$800-$1,000

1059
$1,000-$1,200

1394
$1,000-$1,300

1717
$1,000-$1,200

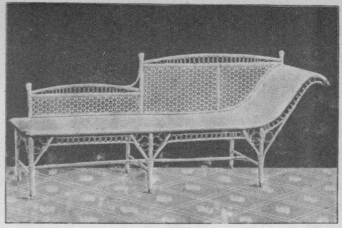

1690
$950-$1,350

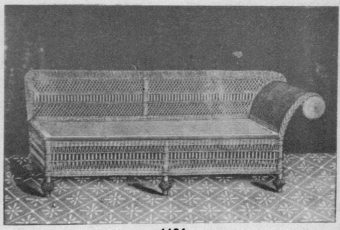

1164
$1,000-$1,450

54
$900-$1,250

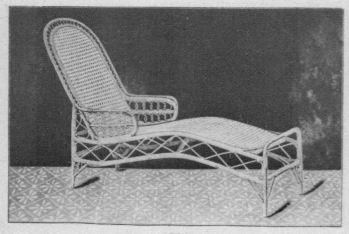

55
$900-$1,250

3161
$1,100-$1,500

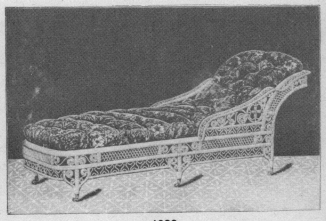

1099
$1,250-$1,650

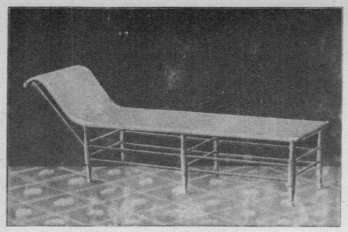

1549
$500-$700

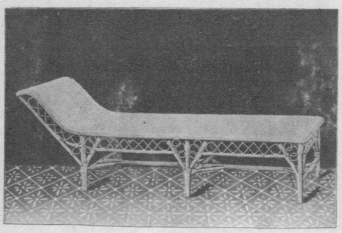

345
$750-$950

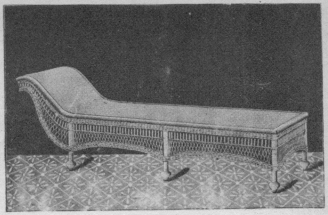

956
$900-$1,200

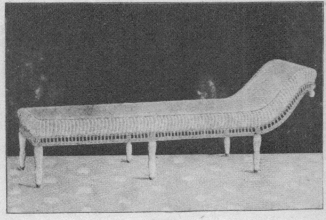

3055
$900-$1,200

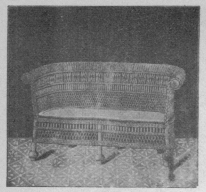

1449
$750-$950

907
$900-$1,200

1439
$750-$950

3054
$750-$1,000

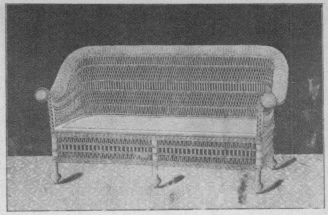

1132
$950-$1,200

Round Hamper
$75-$150

Square Hamper
$85-$165

CATALOGUES OF

CHILDREN'S CARRIAGES

AND

SWINGING SUMMER DOORS

FURNISHED ON APPLICATION.

HEADQUARTERS

FOR

CHAIR CANE

OF

EVERY WIDTH AND GRADE.

Carriage.	Narrow Binding.	No. 5 Flat Pith.
Superfine.	No. 1 Binding.	No. 5 1-2 Flat Pith.
Fine Fine.		No. 6 1-2 Flat Pith.
Fine.	"A" Wide Binding.	No. 8 Flat Pith.
Narrow Medium.	"B" Wide Binding.	No. 5 Oval Pith.
Medium.		No. 5 1-2 Oval Pith.
Wide Medium.	"C" Wide Binding.	No. 6 1-2 Oval Pith.
Common.		

Price List and Sample Cards furnished on Application.

VICTORIAN WICKER FURNITURE

Now considered the Golden Age of Wicker, the ornate styles of the Victorian era (1837 - 1901) were perfectly suited to the elastic properties of wicker furniture. The late 19th century penchant for lavish and often gaudy furniture was met head-on by the fledging wicker furniture industry in America. It simply came along at the right time and filled a need. It was both romantic and exotic.

While virtually all Victorian furniture revived the many historical styles of the past, wicker furniture from this era was an especially dramatic mixture of progressive, experimental designs and the successful adaptation of such antiquarian styles as Rococo (Louis XIV), Elizabeth (Tudor and Jacobean), Chinese, Classical, Italian Renaissance and Gothic. However, where there was a tremendous variety of wicker designs that emerged during this period, it should be noted that the majority of pre-1870 wicker was more often than not simple in design. In fact, it wasn't until after the Civil War that wicker manufacturers adapted their designs in order to capitalize on the Victorian fetish for elaborate scrollwork and flowing designs. Ultimately, these Victorian excesses led to woven back panels for armchairs and rockers which utilized such unusual motifs as banjoes, hearts, feathers, leaves, sailboats, liberty bells and even American flags!

BASKETS

☐ **1 Sewing Basket,** natural
finish,
c 1880's . . **165.00 225.00**
Credit: The Collected Works

☐ **2 Sewing Basket,** natural
finish, bentwood handle,
baskets are finished off
with reed braidwork,
Wakefield Rattan
Company,
c 1890's . . **200.00 275.00**
Credit: Wacky Wicker Workers

☐ **3 Sewing Basket,** natural finish, closely woven lid on hinges, c 1890's ... **275.00   350.00**

☐ **4 Sewing Basket,** natural finish, loop design on bottom shelf, crisscross weave on basket, c 1880's .. **250.00   325.00**

Credit: The Wicker Lady

☐ **5 Sewing Basket,** natural
finish, rare curlicue and
spool design on basket,
large birdcage design at
middle of brace, Wakefield
Rattan Company,
c 1880's . . **300.00   425.00**
Credit: The Wicker Porch

☐ **6 Sewing Basket,** natural
finish, spiderweb caned
top basket and lower shelf,
three legged design, cir-
cular hinged lid,
c. 1870's . . **275.00   350.00**
Credit: Circa 1890's

☐ **7 Sewing Basket,** natural finish, swinging boat-shaped main compartment, hinged top, circular basket at mid level used for a pin cushion, reed bottom shelf, graceful and unique design throughout, c. 1890's .. **275.00   350.00**
Credit: A Summer Place

☐ **8 Sewing Basket,** rare, natural finish, unique camel's back lid, extremely fancy wickerwork throughout, c. 1890's. 475.00   625.00
Credit: Hays House of Wicker

☐ **9 Sewing Basket,** natural finish, Wakefield Rattan Company, c 1890's . **165.00   225.00**
Credit: Wacky Wicker Workers

☐ **10 Sewing Basket,** painted light blue and gilded beadwork at the factory, circular bottom shelf, hinged top, Heywood Brothers and Company, c 1890's .. **350.00   450.00**

☐ **11 Sewing Basket,** white, spiderweb caning on basket and hinged lid, Wakefield Rattan Company, c 1890's . . **175.00 245.00**

☐ **12 Wood Basket,** natural finish, loop motif set into circular design, closely woven tray, ball feet, c 1890's . .**135.00 195.00**
Credit: The Willow Tree

☐ **13 Wood Basket,** white, 12″ x
18″, closely woven reed
bottom,
c 1890's .. **125.00   165.00**
Credit: The Wicker Garden

BOOKCASES

☐ **1 Bookshelf,** natural finish,
four oak shelves, turned
wood frame, reed and
wood fancywork at top,
c 1890's .. **500.00   750.00**
Credit: The Wicker Lady

☐ **2 Whatnot,** natural finish, four oak-topped tiers, wrapped ball design throughout, c. 1880's . . **800.00 950.00**
Credit: A Summer Place

☐ **3 Whatnot,** natural finish, 7′ high, extremely rare, unique "corner" design, five oak shelves, extensive fancywork, c 1880's . . **2200.00 +**
Credit: House of Wicker

☐ **4 Whatnot,** natural finish,
28″ x 60″, very rare, called
a "fancy cabinet" in
Victorian trade catalogues,
Heywood Brothers and
Company,
c 1890's .. **1400.00 1800.00**
Credit: The Wicker Lady

☐ **5 Whatnot,** white, elongated
birdcage design decorates
legs, four tiers,
c 1890's .. **650.00 850.00**
Credit: The Wicker Garden

☐ **6 Whatnot,** white, four-tier design, very unique shaped middle shelves, also unconventional wooden beadwork throughout, c 1880's . . **1000.00 1500.00**
Credit: Wacky Wicker Workers

☐ **7 Whatnot,** white, pineapple motif in back is the symbol of hospitality, four oak shelves, c 1890's . . **285.00 395.00**
Credit: A Summer Place

CARRIAGES

☐ **1 Baby Carriage,** natural finish, elegantly simple
flowing design, wooden wheels, c 1880's **600.00   750.00**
Credit: Hays House of Wicker

☐ **2 Baby Carriage,** natural
finish, rolled arms and
back, unique star-
shaped design on sides,
wooden spoked wheels,
c 1880's   **500.00   650.00**

☐ **3 Baby Carriage,** natural finish, serpentine edges, original velveteen upholstery, c 1890's . .   **500.00**   **650.00**
Credit: Wacky Wicker Workers

☐ **4 Baby Carriage,** natural finish, serpentine edges, wooden wheels, elliptical front and back springs, c 1890's 450.00   600.00
Credit: Hays House of Wicker

☐ **5 Baby Carriage,** natural finish, spiderweb caned side panels, runners for winter use were sold separately by the manufacturer, Heywood Brothers and Company, c 1880's 550.00   675.00

☐ **6 Baby Carriage,** natural finish, unique side han-
dles, Wakefield Rattan Company, c 1890's **650.00   775.00**
Credit: Wacky Wicker Workers

☐ **7 Baby Carriage,** natural finish, wooden beadwork, set-in caned bottom, metal wheels,
parasol, c. 1890's........................... **500.00   650.00**
Credit: The Collected Works

☐ **8 Baby Carriage,** white, elaborate use of curlicues, rubber tires, Heywood Brothers and Company, c 1880's 400.00   575.00

☐ **9 Baby Carriage,** white, flowing scrollwork, set-in
caned bottom, adjustable back, brass label
reads "The Heywood Sleeper," Heywood
Brothers and Company, c 1890's 600.00   750.00

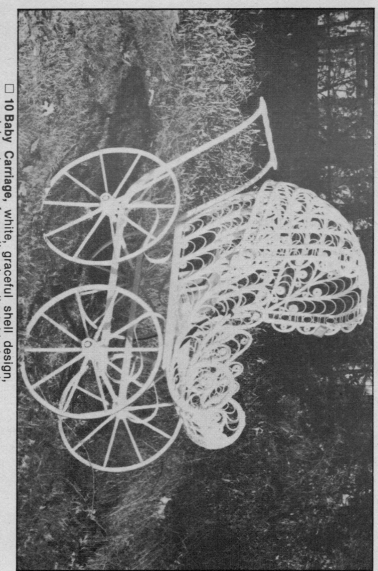

☐ **10 Baby Carriage,** white, graceful shell design, elaborate use of scrollwork, adjustable hood, wooden wheels, made by the F.A. Whitney Carriage Company, c. 1880's ....
Credit: The Wicker Porch

650.00   785.00

☐ **11 Baby Carriage,** white, rare use of wooden bead-work set into closely woven side panels and front, Heywood Brothers and Company, c 1890's 600.00 725.00
Credit: The Collected Works

☐ **12 Twin Baby Carriages,** natural finish, extremely rare, two seats face each other, double parasols, Heywood Brothers and Wakefield Company, c. 1890's **700.00   950.00**

CHAIRS

☐ **1 Armchair,** white, extemely rare, hand caned square backrest, seat lifts up and unfolds to create full-length lounge, c 1880's .. **1600.00** +
Credit: A Summer Place

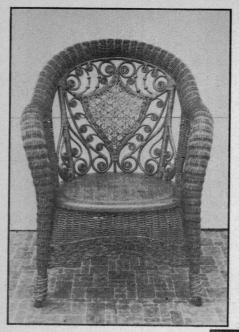

☐ **2 Armchair,** natural finish, caned shield back panel, serpentine edges, Whitney Reed Chair Company, c 1890's . . **400.00 550.00**
Credit: Wacky Wicker Workers

☐ **3 Armchair,** natural finish, circular reed seat, c 1890's . . **275.00 375.00**

☐ **4 Armchair,** natural finish,
rolled arms, wooden bead-
work, curlicues, set-in cane
seat,
c 1890's .. **350.00 425.00**
Credit: Arabesque Antiques

☐ **5 Armchair,** natural finish,
leather back panel and
seat are not original and
therefore diminish the
value,
c 1890's .. **200.00 275.00**
*Credit: Montgomery Auction
Exchange*

☐ **6 Armchair,** natural finish,
rare Edwardian
gentleman's chair, spiderweb caned circular top
panel and curved lower
back panel,
c 1880's .. **500.00 650.00**
Credit: Wacky Wicker Workers II

☐ **7 Armchair,** natural finish, serpentine arms and back, ball feet, c 1890's .. **475.00 600.00**
Credit: The Wicker Porch

☐ **8 Armchair,** natural finish, odd square-shaped design at the lower back and elaborate beadwork in center panel, c 1890's .. **450.00 550.00**
Credit: Montgomery Auction Exchange

☐ **9 Armchair,** natural finish, unique head rest, extensive use of curlicue design, c 1890's **300.00 400.00**
Credit: Montgomery Auction Exchange

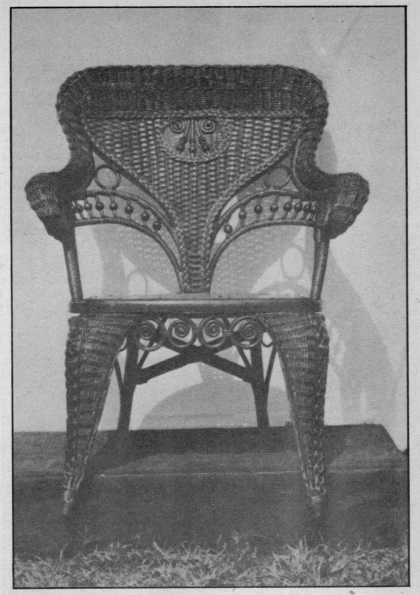

☐ **10 Armchair,** natural finish, unique triangular-shaped woven front legs, c 1890's **400.00   500.00**
Credit: The Wicker Porch

☐ **11 Armchair,** natural finish, this very popular serpentine shell-back design is now being reproduced in several Central and South American countries and imported into the United States. While variations of this particular design dates back to the 1880's, this piece has an authentic "Heywood Brothers and Wakefield Company" red paper label, c 1898-1905 . . . **600.00 750.00**
Credit: The Wicker Porch

☐ **12 Armchair,** natural finish, uniquely intricate design which employs fine criss-cross wickerwork woven into the rolled back and arms, wooden beadwork, birdcage legs and flower motif under seat, c 1890's . . **575.00 700.00**
Credit: Montgomery Auction Exchange

☐ **13 Armchair,** white, closely
woven design with ram's
horn design under arms,
c 1890's . . **675.00 750.00**
Credit: The Wicker Garden

☐ **14 Armchair,** white, flowing
leaf-shaped back panel,
unique mixture of serpen-
tine arm and closely woven
flat arm,
c 1890's . . **400.00 575.00**
Credit: "A Summer Place"

☐ **15 Armchair,** white, odd combination of several styles,
c 1880's . . **350.00 450.00**
Credit: The Wicker Garden

☐ **16 Armchair,** white, odd
square-shaped design at
the lower back and
elaborate beadwork in
center panel,
c 1890's .. **450.00 550.00**
Credit: The Wicker Porch

☐ **17 Armchair,** white, Oriental sea grass woven
over binder cane,
c 1880's **250.00 350.00**

☐ **18 Armchair,** white, modified
butterfly design,
c 1880's .. **275.00 375.00**
Credit: House of Wicker

☐ **19 Armchair,** white, rolled back and arms, circular skirting under seat employs some fancywork, c 1890's **300.00**   **425.00**
Credit: Montgomery Auction Exchange

☐ **20 Armchair,** white, serpentine edges and closely woven reed back panel, c 1890's **250.00**   **325.00**
Credit: The Wicker Porch

☐ **21 Armchair,** white, serpentine back and arms, elaborate fancywork, set-in cane seat,
c 1880's .. **275.00 395.00**
Credit: The Wicker Lady

☐ **22 Armchair,** white, serpentine back and arms, inverted triangle design woven into back, Heywood Brothers and Company,
c 1890's .. **400.00 500.00**
Credit: Lightfoot House

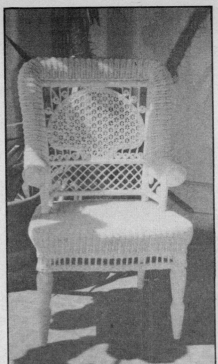

☐ **23 Armchair,** white, serpentine arms and back, mushroom design set into back panel, c 1890's . . **400.00 500.00**
Credit: Lightfoot House

☐ **24 Armchair,** white, serpentine back and arms, ram's horn curls under set-in cane seat, birdcage legs and ball feet, c 1890's . . **550.00 675.00**
Credit: The Wicker Lady

☐ **25 Armchair,** white, serpentine back and arms, scalloped design woven into backrest and skirting, Heywood Brothers and Company, c. 1890's . . **450.00 600.00**
Credit: Joan M. Cole Wicker

☐ **26 Armchair,** white, serpentine edges, rosettes at arm tips, set-in cane seat, c 1890's .. **475.00 650.00**
Credit: Lightfoot House

☐ **27 Armchair,** white, serpentine back and arms, wooden beadwork under arms and seat, graceful scrollwork under arms, c 1890's .. **250.00 350.00**
Credit: The Wicker Lady

☐ **28 Armchair,** white, very popular Victorian design, Gendron Iron Wheel Company, c 1880's .. **350.00 475.00**
Credit: The Wicker Porch

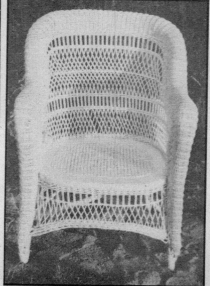

☐ **29 Child's Invalid Chair,** extremely rare, natural
finish, wooden footrest and wheels, hand-
caned seat, c. 1870's **225.00   335.00**
Credit: Wickering Heights

☐ **30 Conversation Chair,**
natural finish, extremely
rare square-backed design,
wooden beadwork set into
lower backs, ball feet,
serpentine backs,
c 1890's . . **1000.00 1500.00**
Credit: The Wicker Lady

☐ **31 Conversation Chair,** natural finish, rolled closely woven backs, curlicue design, birdcage
design adorns posts, dual set-in cane seats,
c. 1890's **1300.00   1700.00**
Credit: A Summer Place

☐ **32 Conversation Chair,** white, Heywood Brothers
and Company, c 1880's **750.00   950.00**
Credit: Montgomery Auction Exchange

☐ **33 Corner Chair,** natural finish, extremely ornate and rare, note birdcage arms and elaborate fancy-work on legs, c 1880's . . **600.00 700.00**
Credit: Hays House of Wicker

☐ **34 Corner Chair,** natural finish, fancy scrollwork, Heywood Brothers and Company, c 1890's . . **600.00 700.00**
Credit: Wacky Wicker Workers

☐ **35 Corner Chair,** natural finish, rolled back, curlicues and criss-cross design set into back, c 1890's . . **450.00 575.00**
Credit: Montgomery Auction Exchange

☐ **36 Corner Chair,** natural
finish, rolled armrest,
wooden beadwork, set-in
cane seat,
c 1890s . . . **575.00 700.00**
Credit: Wacky Wicker Workers

☐ **37 Corner Chair,** natural
finish, rolled back, rosette
arm tips, flat woven reed
seat,
c 1890's .. **550.00 675.00**
*Credit: Montgomery Auction
Exchange*

☐ **38 Corner Chair,** natural finish, serpentine back and arms, unique birdcage design and curlicues set into middle leg, J.A. Dickerman & Company, c 1890s . . . **550.00 675.00**
Credit: Wacky Wicker Workers

☐ **39 Corner Chair,** natural finish, unique circular flower motif dominates the design, c 1880's . . **575.00 685.00**
Credit: Cubbyhole Antiques

☐ **40 Corner Chair,** natural finish, very ornate, extensive use of wooden beads, c 1880's .. **600.00 750.00**
Credit: House of Wicker

☐ **41 Corner Chair,** white, rare woven triangular seat, birdcage legs, c 1890's .. **450.00 525.00**
Credit: Lightfoot House

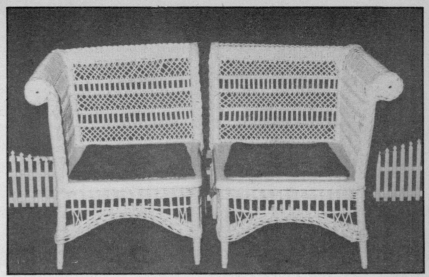

☐ **42 Corner Chairs,** white, rare pair can form an im-
promptu settee, for the pair, c 1890's **650.00   900.00**
Credit: Cubbyhole Antiques

☐ **43 Corner Chair,** white,
serpentine back and arm,
closely woven back panel
with unique beadwork
design,
c 1890's . . **450.00 600.00**
*Credit: Windsor's Cane
& Wicker Repair*

☐ **44 Corner Chair,** white,
serpentine back, hand-
caned back panel, set-in
cane seat,
c 1880's . . **425.00 550.00**
Credit: The Wicker Lady

□ **45 Corner Chair,** white, serpentine back, wrapped ball design, note fancywork covering ball feet,
c 1890's **525.00 650.00**
Credit: Wacky Wicker Workers

□ **46 Corner Chair,** white, triangular back panel, rosette arm tip,
c 1890's **450.00 600.00**
Credit: Cubbyhole Antiques

☐ **47 Corner Chair,** white,
serpentine back, woven flat
reed seat, rosette arm tips,
c 1890's . . **550.00 675.00**
Credit: The Wicker Garden

☐ **48 Fancy Exposition Chair,**
natural finish, extremely
rare, this odd design is
actually a cross between a
corner chair and a Turkish
chair, elaborate birdcage
legs, thick scrollwork
under closely woven reed
seat, wooden beadwork
under arms,
c 1880's . . **900.00 1350.00**
*Credit: Windsor's Cane
& Wicker Repair*

☐ **49 Fancy Chair,** white, most often used as a photographer's chair, extremely ornate, note four rows of wooden beadwork in backrest and octopus-like scrollwork at bottom right, Wakefield Rattan Company,
c 1890's   **675.00   850.00**
Credit: The Wicker Garden

☐ **50 High Chair,** natural finish, flowing shell design for backrest, turned wood legs, wooden footrest, set-in cane seat,
c 1880's . .   **250.00   350.00**
Credit: Joan M. Cole Wicker

☐ **51 High Chair,** natural finish, serpentine back and arms, footrest, c 1890's . . **275.00 375.00**
Credit: The Wicker Garden

☐ **52 High Chair,** white, closely woven back panel is divided by reed braiding, wooden footrest, c 1890's . . **250.00 325.00**

☐ **53 High Chair,** white, complete with wooden tray and footrest,
c 1880's . **275.00 375.00**
Credit: Hays House of Wicker

☐ **54 High Chair,** white, lift-up wooden tray, wooden footrest, hand caned back panel, set-in cane seat,
c 1890s . . . **245.00 320.00**
Credit: Arabesque Antiques

☐ **55 High Chair,** white, serpentine back, set-in cane seat, c 1890's . . **235.00 300.00**
Credit: The Wicker Garden

☐ **56 Photographer's Chair,** white, mushroom-shaped back panel is outlined with fancywork and curlicue designs, closely woven armrest, c 1890's **700.00 850.00**
Credit: Montgomery Auction Exchange

☐ **57 Photographer's Chair,**
natural finish, the famous
"prop" chair used in Vic-
torian studio portrait
photography, extremely ornate, extensive scrollwork,
c 1880's . . **750.00 1000.00**
Credit: The Collected Works

☐ **58 Photographer's Chair,**
white, an extremely rare
and elaborate design,
extraordinary number of
curlicues outline the back
panel, built-in bud vase
platform at top right,
c 1890's . . **1400.00 +**
Credit: The Collected Works

☐ **59 Posing Chair,** white, rare,
this unique design was
produced specifically for
commercial studio
photographers as props,
note elaborate use of
curlicues and five-leg
design,
c 1890's . . **500.00 650.00**
*Credit: Montgomery Auction
Exchange*

☐ **60 Side Chair,** natural finish, a fine example of what was called a "Lady's Reception Chair" in Victorian era wicker trade catalogues, c 1880's .. **285.00 385.00**
Credit: Connecticut Wholesale Wicker

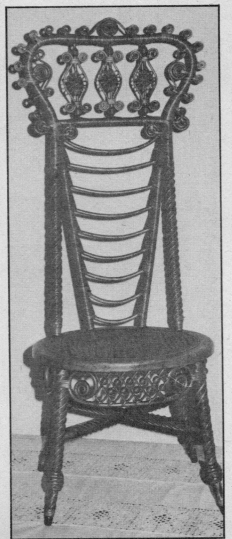

☐ **61 Side Chair,** natural finish, adaptation of the colonial ladder-back design, very ornate fancywork worked into top of the back panel, hand caned seat, Heywood Brothers and Company, c 1880's .. **450.00 600.00**
Credit: Cubbyhole Antiques

☐ **62 Side Chair,** natural finish, amazingly intricate weaving and unique use of wooden beadwork set into the back, c 1880's **385.00   485.00**
Credit: The Wicker Garden

☐ **63 Side Chair,** natural finish, birdcage design on posts and legs, wooden beadwork, Heywood Brothers and Wakefield Company, c 1890's . . **225.00 325.00**
Credit: Wacky Wicker Workers

☐ **64 Side Chair,** natural finish, closely woven back panel utilizes scalloped design at center, closely woven shields cover each leg, Heywood Brothers and Wakefield Company, c 1890s . . . **235.00 300.00**
Credit: Wacky Wicker Workers

☐ **65 Side Chair,** natural finish, dual flower designs woven into back rest, generous use of wooden beadwork and curlicues, figure-eight design adorns front legs, c 1890's .. **325.00 400.00**
Credit: Montgomery Auction Exchange

☐ **66 Side Chair,** natural finish, closely woven circular seat, unique use of circle design in graduated sizes, wooden beadwork, c 1890's .. **260.00 350.00**
Credit: Joan M. Cole Wicker

☐ **67 Side Chair,** natural finish, closely woven oval back panel, rolled edges, set-in cane seat, Whitney Chair Company, c 1890's . . **225.00 350.00**
Credit: Wacky Wicker Workers

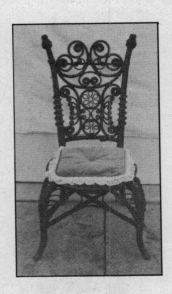

☐ **68 Side Chair,** natural finish, clover design set into round pieces in backrest, cabriole legs, c 1890s . . . **200.00 285.00**
Credit: Wacky Wicker Workers

□ **69 Side Chair,** natural finish, extensive use of curlicues and beadwork, set-in cane seat, Heywood Brothers and Wakefield Company, c 1890's . . **235.00 325.00**
Credit: Wacky Wicker Workers

□ **70 Side Chair,** natural finish, extensive use of scrollwork, cabriole legs, Whitney Chair Company, c 1890's . . **295.00 350.00**
Credit: Wacky Wicker Workers

□ **71 Side Chair,** natural finish, graceful back panel dominates this piece, wooden beadwork, cabriole legs, set-in cane seat, c 1880's . . **225.00 325.00**
Credit: Joan M. Cole Wicker

☐ **72 Side Chair,** natural finish, heart-shaped design dominates backrest, generous use of curlicues, cabriole legs, c 1880's .. **185.00 275.00**
Credit: Montgomery Auction Exchange

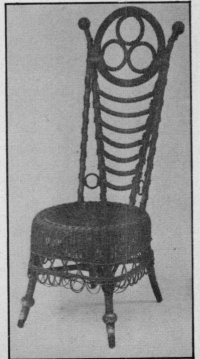

☐ **73 Side Chair,** natural finish, ladder-back design is colonial in origin, c 1890's .. **275.00 325.00**
Credit: The Collected Works

☐ **74 Side Chair,** natural finish, rare mixture of curlicues and closely woven back panel, c 1890's .. **175.00 250.00**
Credit: The Wicker Porch

☐ **75 Side Chair,** natural finish, spider web hand caning set into circular backrest, set-in cane seat, c 1890's .. **225.00 300.00**
Credit: Montgomery Auction Exchange

☐ **76 Side Chair,** natural finish, unconventional woven round seat flows into legs, diamond-shaped beadwork set into back, c 1890's **260.00   350.00**
Credit: The Wicker Garden

☐ **77 Side Chair,** natural finish, unique backrest utilizes wooden beadwork and curlicues, cathedral spire back braces, c 1880's . . **250.00 350.00**
Credit: Montgomery Auction Exchange

☐ **78 Side Chair,** natural finish, tall back employs cane-wrapped squares, birdcage design on back and legs, horizontally woven seat of reed, c 1880's . . **200.00 285.00**
Credit: Montgomery Auction Exchange

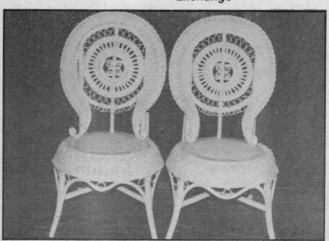

☐ **79 Side Chairs,** white, a rare matching pair, note circular beaded backrests and rolled serpentine edges, for the pair, c 1890's **700.00 900.00**

☐ **80 Side Chair,** white, cabriole legs and caned diamond design set into backrest, c 1880's .. **185.00 275.00**
Credit: The Wicker Porch

☐ **81 Side Chair,** white, beautifully woven ram's horn design and thick curlicues dominate this unique piece, c 1890's .. **200.00 325.00**
Credit: House of Wicker

☐ **82 Side Chairs,** white, extremely rare matching set of four, shell-back design, wooden beadwork, for the set, c 1880's **1500.00 2000.00**
Credit: The Wicker Garden

☐ **83 Side Chair,** white, hand-caned back panel, fancywork includes birdcage designs, curlicues and sunburst pattern in back rest and below seat, c 1880's .. **225.00 325.00**
Credit: Montgomery Auction Exchange

☐ **84 Side Chair,** white, note the turned wooden legs that simulate wrapped cane binding, c 1890's .. **200.00 300.00**

☐ **85 Side Chairs,** white, matching pair, peacock-shaped backs, elongated birdcage legs, for the pair, c 1880's **850.00 1250.00**
Credit: Cubbyhole Antiques

☐ **86 Side Chair,** white, note the wide Oriental sea grass wrapping over previously cane-wrapped back braces and upper legs, c 1890's . . **275.00 375.00**
Credit: The Wicker Garden

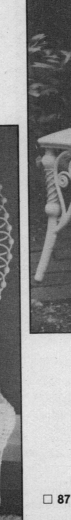

☐ **87 Side Chair,** white, rare cameo-shaped back panel with wooden bead trim, c 1890's . . **235.00 350.00**
Credit: The Wicker Garden

☐ **88 Side Chair,** white, rare full-circle shell-back design, circular woven reed seat, c 1880's . . **350.00 400.00**
Credit: The Wicker Porch

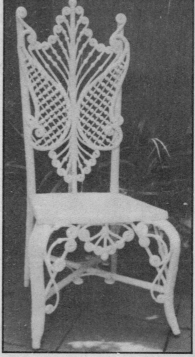

☐ **89 Side Chair,** white, rare wooden-beaded butterfly design dominates this piece, c 1880's . . **225.00 325.00**

☐ **90 Side Chair,** white, spider-web hand caning set into circular backrest, c 1890's .. **235.00 350.00**
Credit: The Wicker Garden

☐ **91 Side Chair,** white, the leaf design set into the back panel is adorned with curlicues, set-in cane seat, c 1800's .. **175.00 275.00**
Credit: The Wicker Porch

☐ **92 Turkish Chair,** white, curlicues and wooden beadwork, c 1890's **325.00** **450.00**
Credit: House of Wicker

☐ **93 Turkish Chair,** white, often used as vanity benches, closely woven reed seat employs diamond design in center, rolled arms, extensive use of curlicues, c 1890's **300.00** **385.00**
Credit: Wacky Wicker Workers

☐ **94 Turkish Chair,** natural finish, closely woven arms and seat, wooden beadwork under arms and seat, c 1890's .. **325.00 400.00**
Credit: Montgomery Auction Exchange

☐ **95 Vanity Chair,** natural finish, serpentine back, rectangular spiderweb caned back panel, circular woven reed seat, front legs on casters, c 1890's .. **225.00 350.00**
Credit: Hays House of Wicker

CRIBS

☐ **1 Standing Crib,** natural finish, rare "drop-side" panel shown in second photo, flower motif set into headboard, Wakefield Rattan Company, c 1870's 1200.00 1500.00

Credit: Cubbyhole Antiques

☐ **2 Standing Crib,** natural finish, unique spiderweb caned oval panels, Wakefield Rattan Company, c 1880's **750.00   1000.00**
Credit: Montgomery Auction Exchange

☐ **3 Swinging Crib,** natural finish, elaborate fancywork, canopy, Wakefield Rattan Company, c 1890's **1000.00 1400.00**
Credit: A Summer Place

☐ **4 Swinging Crib,** natural finish, extensive use of curlicues, Heywood Brothers and Company, c 1880's 850.00 1100.00
Credit: The Wicker Lady

☐ **5 Standing Crib,** white, scrollwork atop canopy brace and under cradle frame, wooden beadwork worked into cradle, c 1890s 700.00 825.00
Credit: Calendar Court Antiques

DOLL BUGGY

☐ **1 Doll Buggy,** white, 35″
long, metal wheels, turned
wooden beadwork
attached to tips of reeds,
arched metal parasol
holder, canvas parasol,
c 1880's . . **325.00 435.00**

☐ **2 Doll Buggy,** natural finish,
32″ long, wickerwork
emphasizes flowing
design, silk parasol,
wooden wheels, metal
rims,
c 1880's . . **350.00 450.00**
*Credit: Windsor's Cane & Wicker
Repair*

HANGING MUSIC RACKS

☐ **1 Hanging Music Rack,** natural finish, rare, elabo-
rate scrollwork, c 1880's **225.00   350.00**
Credit: The Wicker Lady

LOUNGES

☐ **1 Lounge,** natural finish, rare upholstered design, c 1890's **1000.00 1600.00**
Credit: House of Wicker

☐ **2 Lounge,** natural finish, serpentine back, arms and footrest, set-in cane seat, Heywood Brothers and Wakefield Company, c late 1890's **1000.00 1600.00**
Credit: Wacky Wicker Workers

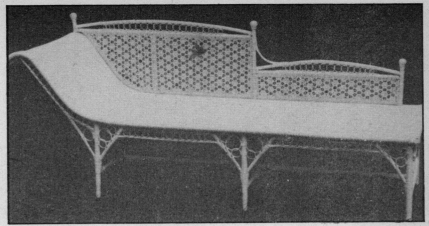

☐ **3 Lounge,** white, hand-caned back panel, seat and backrest are made of closely woven reed matting, loop design at top and under seat, c 1880's **950.00   1400.00**
Credit: The Wicker Lady

☐ **4 Lounge,** white, rolled arm and back, criss-cross design dominates backrest and skirting, ball feet, c 1890's **850.00   1250.00**

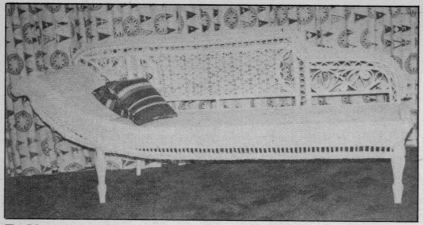

☐ **5 Lounge,** white, rolled back, hand-caned backrest, set-in caned seat, serpentine top roll, c 1890's 1000.00 1300.00
Credit: A Summer Place

ROCKERS

☐ **1 Child's Rocker,** natural finish, circular backrest, unique armrests end in reed-wrapped balls, set-in cane seat, Heywood Brothers and Company, c 1890's .. **185.00 275.00**
Credit: Montgomery Auction Exchange

☐ **2 Child's Rocker,** natural finish, flowing shell design makes up backrest, set-in cane seat, turned wood framework, c 1880's .. **200.00 300.00**
Credit: A Summer Place

☐ **3 Child's Rocker,** natural finish, hand caned back panel, loop design outlines back and arms, Heywood Brothers and Company, c 1880's . . **200.00 285.00**
Credit: Joan M. Cole Wicker

☐ **4 Child's Rocker,** natural finish, serpentine back and arms, wooden beadwork, c 1890's . . **200.00 300.00**
Credit: The Wicker Garden

☐ **5 Child's Rocker,** natural finish, spiderweb caned back panel, upholstered seat not original, c 1880's . . **165.00 235.00**
Credit: Calendar Court Antiques

☐ **6 Child's Rocker,** white, fan
motif woven into back
panel,
c 1880's . . **200.00   300.00**
Credit: The Collected Works

☐ **7 Child's Rocker,** white,
spiderweb caned back
panel, wooden beadwork
under arms,
c 1890's . . **200.00   275.00**
Credit: Hays House of Wicker

☐ **8 Platform Rocker,** natural finish, closely woven and curved headrest, designed to reduce carpet wear, c 1880's **600.00 750.00**
Credit: Wacky Wicker Workers

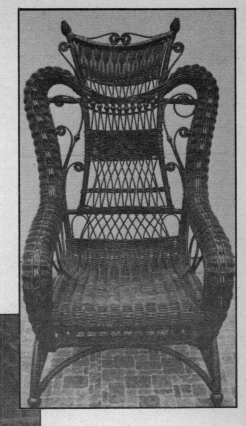

☐ **9 Platform Rocker,** natural finish, curved backrest, serpentine back and arms, c 1890's **525.00 650.00**
Credit: Wisteria Antiques

□ **10 Platform Rocker,** natural finish, rare lyre motif set into back panel, unique horizontal birdcage design under seat, A. H. Ordway & Company, c 1880's **600.00 750.00**
Credit: Wacky Wicker Workers

□ **11 Platform Rocker,** natural finish, fine example of fan motif set into back panel, Wakefield Rattan Company, c 1870's **650.00 775.00**
Credit: The Wicker Porch

☐ **12 Platform Rocker,** natural finish, serpentine headrest and arms, ball feet, closely woven seat, c 1890s 550.00   685.00
Credit: Lightfoot House

☐ **13 Platform Rocker,** natural finish, unique "Turkish dome" design tops each serpentine arm, large metal springs mounted under the rocker and on top of the platform base prevented the sitter from tipping too far backwards, c 1890's .   **600.00   725.00**
Credit: The Wicker Garden

☐ **14 Platform Rockers,** white, extremely rare matching pair, note looped reed design at top, for the pair, c 1880's . . . .   **1200.00 +**
Credit: Lightfoot House

☐ **15 Platform Rocker,** white, serpentine back, arms and arched platform, Heywood Brothers and Company, c 1890's . .   **600.00   750.00**

☐ **16 Platform Rocker,** white, the age of this rather plain design is deceptively old, note the closely woven cane matting covering the platform and rocker, casters in front, c 1870's . .   **585.00   700.00**
Credit: The Collected Works

☐ **17 Rocker,** natural finish, circular loop design around back frames fancy back panel, hand-caned seat, c 1870's .. **350.00 435.00**

☐ **18 Rocker,** natural finish, closely woven back panels separated by wooden beadwork, set-in cane seat, c 1890's .. **450.00 575.00**
Credit: The Wicker Garden

☐ **19 Rocker,** natural finish, deceptively old design, curled arms, loop design, c 1870's 500.00   650.00
Credit: Cubbyhole Antiques

☐ **20 Rocker,** natural finish,
crisscross beadwork,
serpentine back and
arms,
c 1890's **450.00 625.00**

☐ **21 Rocker,** natural finish,
extremely rare, the
"liberty bell" woven into
the back panel is
thought to com-
memorate the Centen-
nial, very unique finely-
braided reed is worked
into the center of the
serpentine edges,
c 1880's **1100.00 +**
*Credit: Windsor's Cane
& Wicker Repair*

☐ **22 Rocker,** natural finish, hand-caned circular back, serpentine back and arms, curlicue design in lower back, set-in cane seat, c 1890's .   **350.00**   **450.00**
Credit: Wacky Wicker Workers

☐ **23 Rocker,** natural finish, leaf motif set into back
panel, hand-caned seat, c 1880's **475.00**   **575.00**
Credit: The Wicker Garden

☐ **24 Rocker,** natural finish, rare, arms gradually flow up into ram's horn design with beadwork in center, elaborate wooden bead designs also worked into back panel and under arms, highly unusual metal "button" at center of chair has wire spokes over which the circular reed seat was woven, c 1880's **650.00 800.00**
Credit: Windsor's Cane & Wicker Repair

☐ **25 Rocker,** natural finish, rare heart-shaped motif set into back panel, loop design outlines back and arms, c 1880's **475.00 625.00**
Credit: A Summer Place

☐ **26 Rocker,** natural finish, rare teardrop wickerwork
woven into lower back, turned wooden knobs,
serpentine arms, c 1890's 500.00   625.00
Credit: Wacky Wicker Workers

☐ **27 Rocker,** natural finish, serpentine back and arms, c 1890's . . **325.00 420.00**
Credit: Wacky Wicker Workers

☐ **28 Rocker,** natural finish, serpentine back and arms, circular reed design set into back panel, figure-eight design under set-in cane seat, c 1890's **300.00 400.00**
Credit: Montgomery Auction Exchange

☐ **29 Rocker,** natural finish, serpentine back and arms flow down legs and curl up under the seat to frame an intricate circular arabesque, scalloped reed fancywork set into back panel, c 1890s 550.00   675.00
Credit: Wacky Wicker Workers

☐ **30 Rocker,** natural finish, spiderweb caned back panel, c 1880's . . **275.00 350.00**
Credit: The Collected Works

☐ **31 Rocker,** natural finish, turned wooden spoolwork set into lower back, c 1890's . . **325.00 400.00**
Credit: Wacky Wicker Workers

☐ **32 Rocker,** natural finish, spiderweb caned back panel outlined with curlicues, rolled arms, c 1880's **450.00 575.00**
Credit: Montgomery Auction Exchange

☐ **33 Rocker,** natural finish, this design was sometimes called a sewing rocker due to its lack of arm rests which enhanced arm movement, backrest employs curlicues and wooden beadwork, c 1890's **275.00 385.00**
Credit: Montgomery Auction Exchange

☐ **34 Rocker,** natural finish,
very ornate design,
wooden beadwork,
c 1880's **500.00 625.00**
*Credit: Connecticut Wholesale
Wicker*

☐ **35 Rocker,** natural finish,
very rare backrest
design, turned wood
framework, Wakefield
Rattan Company,
c 1890's **375.00 500.00**
Credit: Wacky Wicker Workers

☐ **36 Rocker,** painted green, figure-eight reedwork woven into back panel, extensive use of wooden beads, serpentine arms and legs, lyre design under arm rests, c 1890's 450.00   600.00
Credit: Windsor's Cane & Wicker Repair

☐ **37 Rocker,** white, banjo motif set into back panel, loop design on back and arms, c 1880's . . **400.00 575.00**
Credit: Hays House of Wicker

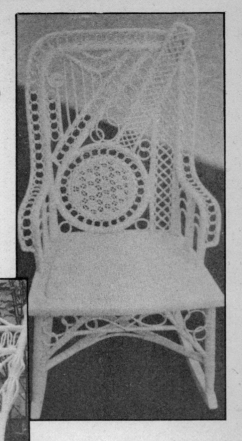

☐ **38 Rocker,** white, circular back panel with spiderweb caning, c 1880's . . **350.00 470.00**
Credit: The Wicker Garden

☐ **39 Rocker,** white, diamond-shaped weave set into circular back panel, wooden beadwork under seat, fancy curlicue skirting, c 1890's **400.00 500.00**
Credit: The Wicker Garden

☐ **40 Rocker,** white, elaborate fancywork dominates this piece, serpentine back, very rare criss-cross design on arms, set-in cane seat, c 1890's **500.00 700.00**
Credit: Windsor's Cane & Wicker Repair

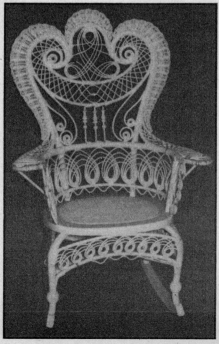

☐ **41 Rocker,** white, four ring design in backrest and "teardrop" arms make this an especially desirable piece,
c 1880's   **450.00   575.00**

☐ **42 Rocker,** white, guitar motif set into back panel, loop design on back and arms, set-in cane seat,
c 1880's   **400.00   600.00**
Credit: The Wicker Lady

☐ **43 Rocker,** white, heart-shaped design set into back, elaborate bird-cage design on legs also employs beadwork, c 1880's **400.00   550.00**
Credit: Hays House of Wicker

☐ **44 Rocker,** white, intricate braidwork decorates the middle of the serpentine back and arms, unique curlicue design covers legs, set-in cane seat, c 1890's **375.00   450.00**
Credit: The Wicker Lady

☐ **45 Rocker,** white, rolled back and
arms, intricate design makes
use of wooden beadwork,
curlicues, birdcage design and
flower motif, set-in cane seat,
c 1880's **650.00 750.00**
Credit: Montgomery Auction Exchange

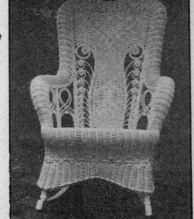

☐ **46 Rocker,** white, inverted
triangular back panel
motif,
c 1890's . . **400.00 550.00**
Credit: The Wicker Garden

☐ **47 Rocker,** white, inverted triangle-shaped back panel employs spiderweb caning, closely woven seat, c 1890's **375.00 475.00**
Credit: The Wicker Lady

☐ **48 Rocker,** white, the circular braidwork on this design is very desirable, spiderweb caned back
panel, c 1880's **400.00   550.00**

☐ **49 Rocker,** white, three-ply crisscross back panel, birdcage designs, c 1890's **350.00 450.00**
Credit: The Wicker Porch

☐ **50 Rocker,** white, unique loop design adorns the top of both arms, spiderweb caned back panel, wooden beadwork, Wakefield Rattan Company, c 1880's **450.00 600.00**
Credit: Windsor's Cane & Wicker Repair

□ **51 Rocker,** white, unusually thick curlicues, turned
wood arm tips, c 1880's 285.00   390.00

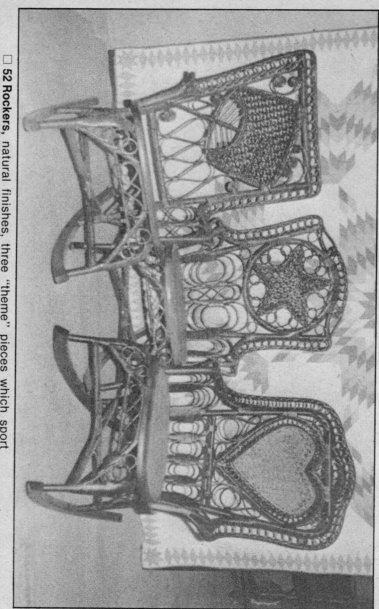

☐ **52 Rockers,** natural finishes, three "theme" pieces which sport various back panel motifs (Japanese fan; star; heart), all have set-in cane seats, c 1880's 475.00 625.00
Credit: A Summer Place

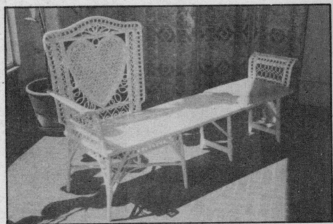

SETS

☐ **1 Armchair-Lounge,** white, extremely rare, heart-shaped back panel with spiderweb caning, three sections unfold to create a full length lounge, c 1880's . . . . **1800.00 +**

Credit: Lightfoot House

☐ **2 Armchair and Matching Footstool,** painted black, hard to find as a set, Heywood Brothers and Company, c 1890 . . . . **700.00 800.00**
Credit: Cubbyhole Antiques

☐ **3 Child's Rocker and High Chair,** natural finishes, both pieces are deceptively old, hand caned seats, Wakefield Rattan Company, c 1870's
High Chair 165.00 235.00
Rocker 120.00 160.00
Credit: Wisteria Antiques

☐ **4 Child's Rocker and High Chair,** natural finishes, matching set, Japanese fan motif woven into backrests, set-in cane seats, c 1880's

Rocker	225.00	325.00
High Chair	300.00	375.00

Credit: A Summer Place

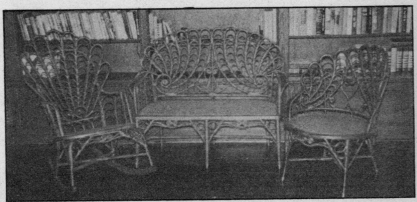

☐ **5 Living Room Set,** matching rocker, settee and corner chair, natural finish, all employ intricate shell design, set-in cane seats, c 1880's .... 2500.00 +
Credit: A Summer Place

☐ **6 Living Room Set,** natural finish, matching sofa and two armchairs, extremely rare set due to age, hand-caned backs and seats, loop design outlines backrests, c 1860s . . . . **3500.00 +**
Credit: A Summer Place

☐ **7 Living Room Set,** natural finish, rare matching set includes corner chair, settee and armchair, hand caned back panels, clover motif inside diamond-shaped top decorations, set-in cane seats, c 1880s . . . . **2500.00 +**
Credit: Circa 1890

☐ **8 Living Room Set**, white, rare seven piece set in the peacock design, heavy use of curlicues and birdcage design, Heywood Brothers & Company, c 1880s .... 3500.00 +
Credit: The Wicker Porch

☐ **9 Rocker and Side Table,** natural finishes, rocker has rare sailboat motif woven into back panel, serpentine back and arms, table employs octagon top and bottom shelf, c 1890s

Rocker . **650.00** **825.00**
Side
Table . . **225.00** **300.00**
Credit: A Summer Place

☐ **10 Settee and Matching Armchair,** natural finishes, hand-caned circular back panels, serpentine backs and arms, set-in cane seats, c 1890's **1250.00** **1700.00**
Credit: A Summer Place

☐ **11 Side Chair and Umbrella Stand,** natural finish, very rare set, unique cattail design, tops of cattails are wrapped with twisted reed, for the set,
c 1890's .. **600.00   850.00**
Credit: A Summer Place

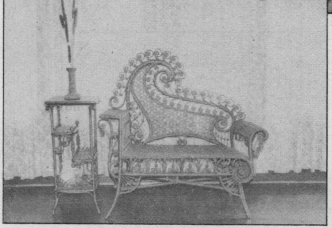

☐ **12 Whatnot Shelf and Divan,** natural finishes, whatnot utilizes oak top and three oak shelves, divan is unique in its elaborate use of scrollwork,
c 1880's

Whatnot	225.00	325.00
Divan	800.00	1000.00

Credit: A Summer Place

SOFAS

☐ **1 Couch,** natural finish, early design of the rarely manufactured three-person piece, loop design outlines arms and three back panels, hand-caned back panels, c 1870's **1000.00   1400.00**
Credit: Montgomery Auction Exchange

☐ **2 Divan,** natural finish, 18″ x 34″, classic Wakefield Rattan Company design, circular sunrise motif set into back, c 1890's **900.00   1350.00**
Credit: Hays House of Wicker

☐ **3 Divan,** natural finish, combination of closely woven reed and wooden beadwork for backrest, serpentine arm and back, set-in cane seat, curlicues on legs, c 1890s 900.00 1150.00
Credit: A Summer Place

☐ **4 Divan,** natural finish, rolled backs and arms employ wooden beadwork, rosette arm tips, set-in cane seat, c 1890's .. 800.00 1000.00
Credit: Montgomery Auction Exchange

☐ **5 Divan,** natural finish, serpentine back, one rolled arm, scalloped wickerwork woven into closely woven back and skirting, curlicues, set-in cane seat, J.A. Dickerman & Company, c 1890s   **800.00   1100.00**
Credit: Wacky Wicker Workers

☐ **6 Divan,** white, elaborate scrollwork and wooden beadwork, figure-eight design in back panel is woven over horizontal weave,
c 1890's . .   **750.00 1000.00**
Credit: Windsor's Cane & Wicker Repair

☐ **7 Divan,** white, exceptionally graceful design utilizes scrollwork and wooden beadwork, serpentine arm and back continues to the floor, birdcage legs, c 1890s **775.00 1000.00**
Credit: Wacky Wicker Workers

☐ **8 Divan,** white, interesting circular beadwork insets under closely woven seat, c 1890's .. **750.00 900.00**
Credit: The Wicker Garden

☐ **9 Divan,** white, serpentine back and arms, heart-shaped back panel outlined by wooden beadwork, Wakefield Rattan Company, c 1880's **800.00**   **1000.00**
Credit: Windsor's Cane & Wicker Repair

☐ **10 Settee,** natural finish, graceful design in its simplicity, curlicues worked into back and under seat, c 1890's **675.00**   **800.00**
Credit: A Summer Place.

☐ **11 Settee,** natural finish, rolled back and arms, odd combination of flowing scrollwork and geometric checkerboard design worked into backrest, c 1890's 750.00   950.00
Credit: Wacky Wicker Workers.

☐ **12 Settee,** natural finish, serpentine back and arms, closely woven back panel, turned wood legs, c 1890's 750.00   900.00
Credit: Wacky Wicker Workers

☐ **13 Settee,** natural finish, very early design, Wake-
field Rattan Company, c 1860's **1300.00   1600.00**
Credit: Cubbyhole Antiques

☐ **14 Settee,** white, example of intricate craftsmanship, rolled back and arms, back panel utilizes
wooden beadwork, closely woven design and
flower motif, birdcage legs, c 1890's **900.00   1300.00**
Credit: Montgomery Auction Exchange

☐ **15 Settee,** white, early wicker design emphasizes reed loops and rustic leg braces, upholstered back covers damaged spiderweb canework, c 1870's 650.00   750.00

☐ **16 Settee,** white, elaborate beadwork creates inverted triangle design in backrest, c 1880's 600.00   750.00
Credit: The Wicker Garden

☐ **17 Settee,** white, peacock design dominates back
panel, birdcage legs, 1880's **950.00   1300.00**
Credit: Cubbyhole Antiques

☐ **18 Settee,** white, rare design employs closely
woven scalloped back woven over exposed vertical spokes, extensive wooden beadwork set
into back and skirting, serpentine arms,
c 1890's **900.00   1250.00**
Credit: Windsor's Cane & Wicker Repair

☐ **19 Settee,** white, rare, round double back panels drip with curlicues, three-leaf design under back panels are woven with Oriental sea grass, c 1880's **950.00 1350.00**
Credit: Cubbyhole Antiques

☐ **20 Settee,** white, rolled back and arms, caned mushroom design set into back panel, c 1890's   **750.00   950.00**
Credit: Montgomery Auction Exchange

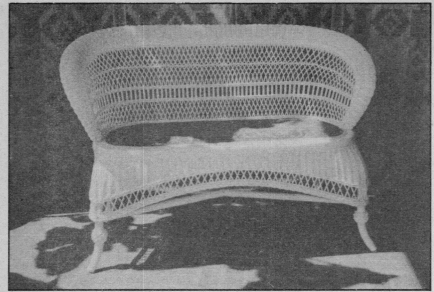

☐ **21 Settee,** white, serpentine design, c 1890's 750.00   950.00
Credit: Lightfoot House

☐ **22 Settee,** white, serpentine back and arms, spiderweb caned back panel, Heywood Brothers and Company, c 1880's 750.00   1000.00

☐ **23 Settee,** white, serpentine shell-back design is a popular wicker reproduction on today's import market, this original piece emphasizes a horseshoe design worked into its closely woven back, c 1890's 900.00   1350.00
Credit: The Wicker Garden

☐ **24 Settee,** white, very ornate scrollwork, Heywood Brothers and Company, c 1880's 900.00   1250.00
Credit: House of Wicker

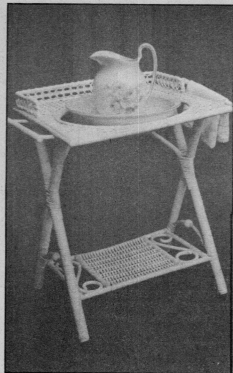

STANDS

☐ **1 Child's Washstand,** white, rare, 21″ x 23″, oval space for wash bowl, towel racks on both sides, closely woven bottom shelf, c 1890's **300.00 425.00**

☐ **2 Music Stand,** natural finish, extremely rare four oak shelves, beveled mirror is adjustable, Wakefield Rattan Company, c 1890's **1800.00 +**
Credit: Hays House of Wicker

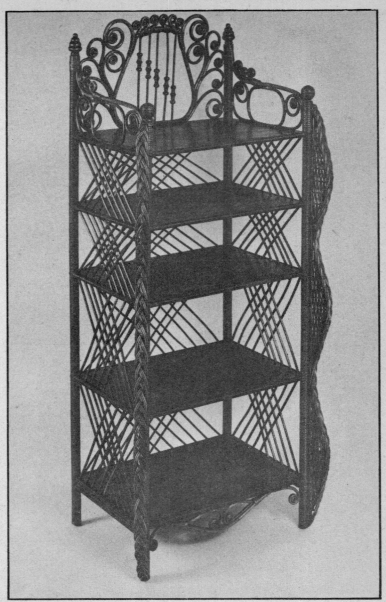

☐ **3 Music Stand,** natural finish, rare, lyre motif at
top embellished with curlicues, reed latticework, thick braiding, turned wood frame,
c 1890's **675.00   900.00**
Credit: The Wicker Garden

☐ **4 Music Stand,** natural
finish, three oak
shelves, Heywood
Brothers and
Company,
c 1890's . **425.00 600.00**
*Credit: Montgomery Auction
Exchange*

☐ **5 Music Stand,** natural
finish, three oak shelves,
Wakefield Rattan
Company,
c 1890's . . **350.00 475.00**
*Credit: Montgomery Auction
Exchange*

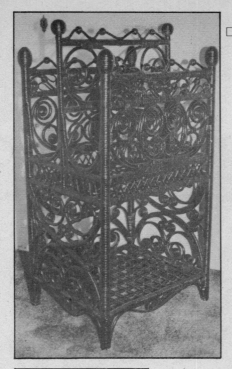

☐ **6 Music Stand,** painted black, two sides for sheet music at top, bottom shelf utilizes checkerboard design, extensive use of curlicues, c 1890s . . . **400.00 550.00**

☐ **7 Music Stand,** white, angled sides, two reed shelves below, ball feet, c 1890's . . **250.00 350.00**

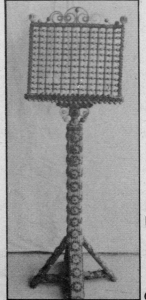

☐ **8 Sheet Music Stand,** natural finish, extremely rare, extensive use of wooden beadwork, woven arabesques decorate base, c 1880s . . . **400.00 +**

Credit: Wacky Wicker Workers

☐ **9 Washstand,** white, very rare, side towel racks, rustic design, tightly woven back, crisscross legs, c 1880's 350.00 500.00
Credit: Cubbyhole Antiques

☐ **10 Washstands,** white, child's size at left employs loop design on rim and ball feet; doll's size at right. Both have side towel racks and lower shelves, c 1890's

Child's	300.00	400.00
Doll's	175.00	275.00

Credit: A Summer Place

STOOLS

☐ **1 Footstool,** natural finish, set-in caned top, wooden beadwork, ball feet, Heywood Brothers and Wakefield Company, c 1890's 135.00   185.00
Credit: Arabesque Antiques

☐ **2 Ottoman,** natural finish, closely woven, seat framed by braidwork, birdcage legs, c 1890's . .   200.00   275.00
Credit: Wacky Wicker Workers

☐ **3 Ottoman,** natural finish, unique crisscross design under top, Wakefield Rattan Company, c 1880's **250.00** **325.00**
Credit: Hays House of Wicker

☐ **5 Ottoman,** white, closely woven top, round rosette design finishes off both ends, c 1890's .. **175.00** **245.00**
Credit: The Wicker Porch

☐ **4 Ottoman,** white, closely woven top and birdcage legs, c 1890's .. **135.00** **190.00**

☐ **6 Piano Stool,** white, 22″ high, rare, circular woven reed seat, c 1890's . . **200.00 285.00**
Credit: The Wicker Garden

TABLES

☐ **1 End Tables,** natural finish, matching pair, very rare as a set, closely woven matting on top and bottom shelves, twisted reed covering on legs, for the pair, c 1880's **900.00 1100.00**
Credit: Cubbyhole Antiques

☐ **2 End Table,** natural finish, closely woven matting covers top and bottom shelf, legs wrapped with twisted round reed, c 1890's .. **300.00 400.00**
Credit: Montgomery Auction Exchange

☐ **3 End Table,** natural finish, graceful design is enhanced by Alladin's slipper legs, square oak top is 16″ in diameter, small bottom shelf is outlined with wooden beadwork, c 1880s **350.00   450.00**
Credit: Joan M. Cole Wicker

☐ **4 End Table,** natural finish, round oak top is a 16″ in diameter, unique use of wooden beadwork on skirting, small oak bottom shelf, c 1890s . . . **375.00   475.00**
Credit: Joan M. Cole Wicker

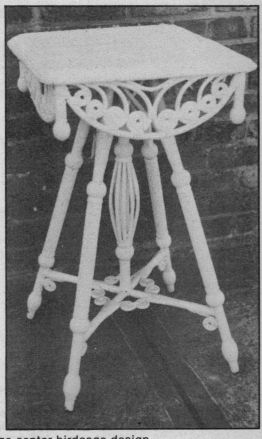

☐ **5 End Table,** white, large center birdcage design is rare, c 1890's **225.00   325.00**
Credit: Wacky Wicker Workers

☐ **6 Library Table,** natural finish, rare, glass top encases dried flowers, curlicues and birdcage legs, c 1880's 950.00   1350.00
Credit: A Summer Place

☐ **7 Oblong Table,** white, oak top and bottom shelf, wooden beadwork set into closely woven skirting, c 1890's 300.00   425.00
Credit: Heirloom Wicker

☐ **8 Oblong Table,** white, wooden beadwork, Chittenden-Eastman Company, c 1890's... **285.00 350.00**

☐ **9 Oblong Table,** white, woven top and bottom shelf, wooden beadwork, c 1890's... **300.00 375.00**
Credit: The Wicker Garden

☐ **10 Oval Table,** natural finish, oak top and bottom
shelf, serpentine design, wooden beadwork,
c 1890's **600.00   800.00**
Credit: A Summer Place

☐ **11 Oval Table,** white, oak top and bottom shelf,
cabriole legs, curlicue design over closely
woven skirting, c 1890's **550.00   700.00**
Credit: The Wicker Lady

☐ **12 Round Table,** white, graceful scalloped skirting, cabriole legs double wrapped with reed and plaited reed finish work, c 1890's **400.00   550.00**
Credit: Montgomery Auction Exchange

☐ **13 Round Table,** white, top is
28″ in diameter, cabriole
legs, wooden beadwork
frames top and bottom
shelf,
c 1890's .. **500.00 750.00**
Credit: Lightfoot House

☐ **14 Side Table,** natural finish,
three-legged design,
triangular oak top and bottom shelf, birdcage design
adorns legs,
c 1890s . . . **250.00 335.00**
Credit: Wacky Wicker Workers

☐ **15 Square Table,** natural finish, combines wooden beadwork, birdcage designs, fancy scrollwork, curlicues, c 1880s **650.00 800.00**
Credit: A Summer Place

☐ **16 Square Table,** natural finish, oak top and bottom shelf, exceptionally intricate weaving is accentuated by fancy colored reeds, Wakefield Rattan Company, c 1890's **750.00 1000.00**
Credit: Montgomery Auction Exchange

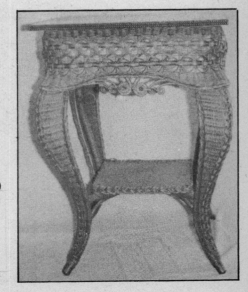

☐ **17 Square Table,** natural finish, oak top, extensive use of birdcage design and curlicues, c 1880's .   **425.00**   **525.00**
Credit: Wacky Wicker Workers

☐ **18 Square Table,** natural finish, 28″ diameter oak top, exceptionally ornate fancywork, cabriole legs, small oak topped bottom shelf, c 1880's ..   **650.00**   **800.00**
Credit: Montgomery Auction Exchange

☐ **19 Square Table,** natural finish, very rare, cane-matted top, oak frame, 104 curlicues, ball feet, c 1880's **600.00   800.00**

☐ **20 Square Table,** white, closely woven top, bead-work set into skirting, c 1880's **300.00   385.00**
Credit: The Wicker Garden

☐ **21 Square Table,** closely
woven flowing skirting
under oak top, wave-like
fancywork at bottom,
Heywood Brothers and
Wakefield Company,
c 1890's ..   **550.00   750.00**
Credit: Heirloom Wicker

☐ **22 Square Table,** white,
twisted reed wrapped
around feet and center
post,
c 1890's ..   **650.00   800.00**
Credit: A Summer Place

MISCELLANEOUS

☐ **1 Doll Bed,** natural finish, extremely rare, loop design adorns sides, bentwood design set into headboard, ball feet on metal casters, c 1880's .   **250.00**   **375.00**
  Credit: The Wicker Lady

☐ **2 Doll Buggy,** natural finish, graceful rolled side design, unique deep footrest, adjustable back, metal wheels, rare original silk parasol, c 1890s   **500.00**   **750.00**
  Credit: Wacky Wicker Workers

☐ **3 Doll Swing,** natural finish, rare, fan motif set into back panel, c 1890's . . **250.00 320.00**
Credit: The Collected Works

☐ **4 Dressing Screen,** gilded, rare, Art Nouveau design utilizes flowing lines, curlicues dominate the inner panels, wooden beadwork at top of each panel, c 1890's **500.00 +**
Credit: Wacky Wicker Workers

☐ **5 Easel,** natural finish, adjustable holder for picture frame, four-leaf clover design set into circle motif,
c 1880's .. **500.00 650.00**
Credit: Wacky Wicker Workers

☐ **6 Easel,** natural finish, rare, very ornate and graceful design for its size at six feet tall,
c 1890's .. **400.00 585.00**
Credit: Circa 1890

7 Easel, white, 74″ high,
curlicue design at top,
c 1890's .. **325.00   425.00**

8 Firescreen, natural finish,
rare, oval center panel is
covered with tapestry,
clover design set into
round sections, loop
design at top,
c 1880's .. **650.00** +
Credit: A Summer Place

☐ **9 Firescreen,** natural finish, rare, spiderweb caned center panel is woven with thin three-ply reed sections, crisscross reed design outlines oval center panel, curlicue design at center, c 1870's .. **500.00 +**

☐ **10 Grandfather's Clock,** white, very rare, 7′ high, unique closely woven base, flower design, wooden beads, curlicues and twisted reed wrapping, c 1890's .. **2500.00 +**

☐ **11 Hanging Shelf,** natural finish, rare, three oak shelves, curlicues at sides and top, c 1890's **225.00 325.00**

☐ **12 Kneeling Bench,** white, very rare, serpentine top, scalloped diamond motif woven into back, c 1890's **500.00 650.00**

☐ **13 Music Cabinet,** natural finish, lyre motif over closely woven compartment door, two sheet music shelves at top, c 1890's **550.00 725.00**
Credit: Circa 1890

☐ **14 Picture Frame,** natural finish, very rare, wooden beadwork and curlicues enhance this most desirable item, c 1890's **250.00 375.00**
Credit: Heirloom Wicker

☐ **15 Swinging Doors,** natural finish, extremely rare, circular glass windows set into closely woven panels, extensive use of curlicues, c 1890's **800.00 +**
Credit: Turn of the Century Antiques

TURN-OF-THE-CENTURY WICKER FURNITURE

The turn-of-the-century was a time of transition in wicker furniture design. While the early 1900s saw the widespread home use of electricity, indoor plumbing and central heating, it was the latter of these improvements that directly affected the wicker furniture industry. Porches all over the country which had utilized wicker for summertime use were now being glassed-in and warmed with the new hot-air heating system. Beyond this, sun rooms and family rooms were also being built at a rapid rate — thus giving these rooms an outdoor feeling while at the same time offering all the modern comforts. Wicker became "the" furniture to use in these "outdoor rooms," as they came to be called.

Wicker styles also underwent dramatic changes from 1900-1920. Although wicker manufacturers continued making Victorian-style pieces until around 1910, extravagantly ornate designs quickly became the exception rather than the rule after the turn-of-the-century. The fact is that many of the late 1890 and early 1900 pieces were being subtly adapted to the onslaught of the "Art Nouveau" style — a school of design which felt that the lines occurring in nature must be the purest and therefore the most beautiful. However, true Art Nouveau wicker was a short-lived phenomenon (1900-1910) simply because it was designed to look as if it were growing out of the floor and therefore closely resembled many of its flowing, ornate Victorian predecessors.

The big change in wicker styles came about as a result of public discontent with the Victorian style in general. Totally rejecting the Victorian and Art Nouveau designs by 1905, Americans sought straight lines and practical styles. Overly fancy wicker was suddenly considered gauche and resigned to the attic. In the meantime the American consumer (for the first time since Cyrus Wakefield began his initial experiments in the 1840s) actively sought wicker made outside of the United States. The reason was simple enough: turn-of-the-century foreign imports from Austria, China and England offered wicker furniture in angular rather than flowing designs.

Finally, with the advent of Gustav Stickley's "Mission" style wicker (sometimes called "Craftsman" furniture) in the early 1900s, the American consumer was offered simple, sturdy looking wicker made in this country. Within five years the wicker industry changed dramatically and functional, straight-lined willow pieces flooded the market. By 1910 extensive fancy-work had all but disappeared.

□ **2 Fernery,** natural finish, thick twisted reed decorative handle, semi-circle design used to fit flat against wall, metal liner, c 1910 . . . .   **85.00   135.00**
Credit: Wacky Wicker Workers

BASKETS

□ **1 Child's Sewing Basket,** orange and black, very rare, 26″ to top to handle, c 1910 . . . .   **150.00   225.00**
Credit: The Collected Works

□ **3 Sewing Basket,** natural finish, closely woven hinged lid, fancywork over horizontal weave, c 1900's . .   **285.00   400.00**
Credit: Hays House of Wicker

☐ **4 Sewing Basket,** natural finish, closely woven, arched lid, wrapped handle, deep bottom shelf, c 1900's **285.00** **375.00**
Credit: Montgomery Auction Exchange

☐ **5 Sewing Basket,** natural finish, hinged lid and body employ woven geometrical cane design, oak topped shelf, cane-wrapped handle, c 1900's . . **275.00 350.00**
Credit: Montgomery Auction Exchange

☐ **6 Sewing Basket,** natural finish, low design did double duty as a footstool, hinged oak top has caned center panel, material can be seen beneath curlicue designs on sides, c 1900's . . **200.00 285.00**
Credit: Montgomery Auction Exchange

☐ **7 Sewing Basket,** natural finish, oval design with wrapped handle, c 1910.... **185.00 250.00**
Credit: Hays House of Wicker

☐ **8 Sewing Baasket,** natural finish, scalloped design in front of basket, wooden hinged lid, wooden shelf, Heywood Brothers and Wakefield Company, c 1900s... **250.00 350.00**
Credit: Wacky Wicker Workers

☐ **9 Sewing Basket,** natural finish, rare canoe-shaped woven basket made of reed, wooden base, c 1900's . . **200.00 285.00**
Credit: Montgomery Auction Exchange

☐ **10 Sewing Basket,** natural finish, turned wood handle and legs, Heywood and Wakefield Company, c 1910 . . . . **200.00 275.00**
Credit: Wacky Wicker Workers

☐ **11 Sewing Basket,** natural finish, unique double lid design, separate compartments for yarn, c 1910 . . . . **250.00 325.00**
Credit: The Collected Works

☐ **12 Sewing Basket,** natural finish, unique drawer under main compartment was used for spool thread, solid oak hinged lid covers yarn basket, oak topped bottom shelf, c 1900s . . . **275.00 375.00**
Credit: A Summer Place

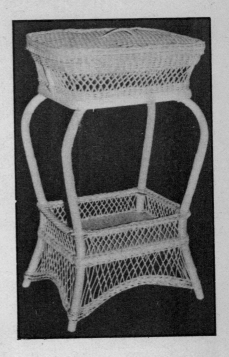

☐ **13 Sewing Basket,** white, lift-
off top, cabriole legs,
c 1900's .. **175.00 250.00**

☐ **14 Sewing Basket,** white,
unique three legged clover-
leaf design, top compart-
ment covered by closely
woven cane matting,
c 1910 .... **225.00 325.00**

☐ **15 Wood Basket,** white, closely woven basket, ball feet, crisscross design, c 1900's .. **135.00   175.00**
Credit: The Wicker Lady

☐ **16 Wood Basket,** natural finish, closely woven Oriental sea grass, reed braidwork, c 1910 .... **95.00   150.00**
Credit: Wisteria Antiques

BOOKCASES

☐ **1 Bookcase,** white, five shelves, wooden beadwork, curlicues at top, c 1910 .... **450.00   650.00**
Credit: Wacky Wicker Workers

☐ **2 Whatnot,** white, closely woven cane matting on four shelves, Heywood Brothers and Wakefield Company, c 1900's .. **300.00   385.00**

CABINETS

☐ **1 Buffet,** natural finish, oak top and two oak
 drawers, two oak-framed glass doors, c 1915 . . **1850.00 +**
Credit: A Summer Place

☐ **2 China Cabinet, natural
 finish, extremely rare, six
 feet high, extensive use of
 wooden beadwork, mir-
 rored top shelf, glass side
 panels, ball feet,
 c 1900s . . . 3500.00 +**
Credit: A Summer Place

☐ **3 Music Cabinet,** white, rare, closely woven top and sides, lyre motif on door, shelves with cubbyholes inside, wrapped cabriole legs,
c 1900's .. **500.00 675.00**

CHAIRS

☐ **1 Armchair,** natural finish, closely woven arms and back, unique design employs continuation of front legs to form handles,
c 1900's .. **250.00 375.00**
Credit: Montgomery Auction Exchange

☐ **2 Armchair,** natural finish, closely woven back and skirting, ball feet, set-in cane seat,
c 1900's .. **375.00 485.00**
Credit: Montgomery Auction Exchange

☐ **3 Armchair,** natural finish, Mission style, closely woven seat, tall openwork sides, ball feet, c 1910 .... **300.00 400.00**
Credit: Wacky Wicker Workers

☐ **4 Armchair,** natural finish, Mission style, distinct angular design woven into backrest, six knobs wrapped with twisted reed, c 1910 .... **375.00 485.00**
Credit: Joan M. Cole Wicker

☐ **5 Armchair,** natural finish,
serpentine edges,
c 1900   **400.00   550.00**
Credit: Wacky Wicker Workers

☐ **6 Armchair,** natural finish,
rolled back and arms,
scalloped design woven
into backrest, birdcage
legs,
c 1900's   **350.00   450.00**
*Credit: Montgomery Auction
Exchange*

☐ **7 Armchair,** natural finish, rolled serpentine back and arms, set-in cane seat,
c 1900's **450.00 585.00**
Credit: Montgomery Auction Exchange

☐ **8 Armchair,** natural finish, unique Mission-influenced design utilizes circular armrests, ball feet,
c 1910 **375.00 475.00**
Credit: The Wicker Porch

☐ **9 Armchair,** white, Bar Harbor design, magazine basket under left arm, ball feet wrapped with Oriental sea grass, Paine Furniture Company,
c 1910   **250.00   350.00**
Credit: The Wicker Porch

☐ **10 Armchair,** white, closely woven design, some fancywork woven into back and under seat,
c 1900's   **375.00   425.00**
Credit: Montgomery Auction Exchange

☐ **11 Armchair,** white, closely
   woven back and skirt-
   ing, ball feet, Heywood
   Brothers and Wakefield
   Company,
   c 1900's **385.00 500.00**
Credit: The Wicker Garden

☐ **12 Armchair,** white, closely
   woven back and skirting,
   rosette design at ends of
   arms, ball feet, Heywood
   Brothers and Wakefield
   Company,
   c 1900's . . **350.00 450.00**
Credit: Cubbyhole Antiques

☐ **13 Armchair,** white, closely woven flat arms, upholstered seat and backrest, Heywood Brothers and Wakefield Company, c 1910 . . . . **300.00 400.00**
Credit: Arabesque Antiques

☐ **14 Armchair,** white, crisscross effect woven into back makes use of three reeds, c 1910 . . . . **260.00 340.00**
Credit: The Wicker Porch

☐ 15 **Armchair,** white, decorative
weaving in middle of
serpentine back and arms,
closely woven back, ball
feet,
c 1900's .. **400.00 500.00**
Credit: The Wicker Lady

☐ 16 **Armchair,** white, rare
"hotel chair" utilizes cylin-
dical walking stick (or umbrella) holder woven into
outside of left arm, magazine holder woven into outside of right arm, Mission
style,
c 1910 .... **450.00 575.00**
Credit: Calendar Court Antiques

☐ **18 Armchair,** white, serpentine back and arms, closely woven design, ball feet, set-in cane seat, Heywood Brothers and Wakefield Company,
c 1900s . . . **250.00 350.00**
Credit: The Wicker Porch

☐ **17 Armchair,** white, rolled arms, scalloped design woven into backrest and skirting, set-in cane seat, c 1900s . . . **350.00 450.00**
Credit: Wacky Wicker Workers

☐ **19 Armchair,** white, serpentine back and arms, closely woven skirting, c 1900's . . **275.00 375.00**

☐ **20 Armchair,** white, serpentine back and arms, intricate wickerwork woven
into lower back panel,
c 1900's .. **500.00 650.00**

☐ **21 Armchair,** white, serpentine back and arms, turned
wood legs,
c 1900's .. **250.00 350.00**

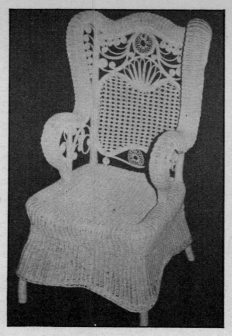

☐ **22 Armchair,** white, unique woven seat, Heywood Brothers and Wakefield Company, c 1900's .. **525.00 650.00**
Credit: House of Wicker

☐ **23 Armchair,** white, willow, classic Bar Harbor design, closely woven seat, ball feet, c 1910 .... **245.00 325.00**
Credit: Wacky Wicker Workers

☐ **24 Armchair,** white, wingback design, magazine
    baskets under both arms, ball feet, c 1910 . . . . .   **325.00   425.00**

☐ **25 Armchair,** white, wingback
    design, upholstered back
    and seat, ball feet,
    c 1915 . . . .   **325.00   425.00**
Credit: The Wicker Porch

☐ **26 Boardwalk Chair,** white, rare, double-seater, metal casters with rubber tires, wooden footrest, possibly made in England, c 1910 . . . .   **900.00 1250.00**

☐ **27 Child's Cabinet Chair,** natural finish, oak seat and tray, closely woven bottom skirting, c 1900's . .   **90.00   125.00**
Credit: Hays House of Wicker

☐ **28 Conversation Chair,** white, rare, handwoven from Oriental sea grass, crisscross reed on arms and back, circular woven seats, c 1900's . .   **600.00   775.00**

□ **29 Corner Chair,** natural
    finish, ball feet,
    c 1900's .. **550.00 700.00**
Credit: Hays House of Wicker

□ **30 Corner Chair,** natural
    finish, heart-shaped motif
    set into back, serpentine
    back, design dates back to
    the Victorian era but was
    continued through the
    turn-of-the-century,
    Heywood Brothers and
    Wakefield Company,
    c 1900's .. **500.00 625.00**
Credit: A Summer Place

☐ **31 Corner Chair,** white, unique five-legged design, ball feet wrapped by twisted reed, set-in cane seat,
c 1900's **450.00 550.00**
Credit: Lightfoot House

☐ **32 High Chair,** natural finish, willow, Bar Harbor design, oak shelf lifts off, ball feet,
c 1915 **160.00 225.00**
Credit: Wacky Wicker Workers

☐ **33 High Chair,** natural finish, wooden tray and footrest, closely woven back, turned wood legs, c 1900's **250.00 325.00**
Credit: The Wicker Porch

☐ **34 High Chair,** white, turned wood legs, braidwork covers top and arms, c 1900's **175.00 250.00**
Credit: The Collected Works

☐ **35 High Chair,** white, wooden tray and footrest, turnedwood legs, closely woven back panel, c 1915 **200.00 275.00**
Credit: The Wicker Garden

☐ **36 Morris Chair,** natural finish, rare, closely woven back and seat, magazine baskets under both arms, adjustable back, c 1905 . . . . **600.00 750.00**

☐ **37 Morris Chair,** natural finish, turned wood framework, closely woven seat, closely woven adjustable backrest employs large diamond design, c 1910 .... 575.00   750.00

□ **38 Side Chair,** natural
  finish, closely woven
  back, turned wood
  frame,
  c 1910 . **175.00   250.00**
Credit: Wacky Wicker Workers

□ **39 Side Chair,** natural
  finish, harp motif at left
  of backrest, set-in cane
  seat,
  c 1900's **175.00   250.00**
*Credit: Montgomery Auction
Exchange*

☐ **40 Side Chairs,** natural finish, matching pair, scrollwork dominates back panels, turned wood legs, set-in cane seats, for the pair, c 1900's **350.00** **525.00**
Credit: The Wicker Garden

☐ **41 Side Chair,** natural finish, rolled back, closely woven back opens to curlicue design at bottom, c 1900's . . **200.00** **275.00**
Credit: Montgomery Auction Exchange

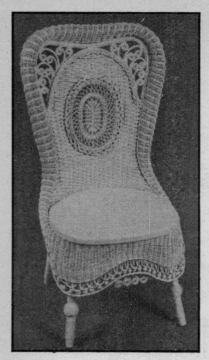

☐ **42 Side Chair,** white, rolled back and arms, oval motif woven into back panel, ball feet,
c 1900's .. **225.00 325.00**
Credit: Montgomery Auction Exchange

☐ **43 Side Chair,** white, closely woven reed seat, framed by braidwork,
c 1910 .... **125.00 180.00**
Credit: Wacky Wicker Workers

☐ **44 Side Chairs,** white, serpentine backs, crescent
moon motif in backs, ball feet, close inspection
reveals they are not a matching pair, both retain
Heywood Brothers and Wakefield Company red
paper labels, for the pair, c 1900's . . . .   **500.00 +**
Credit: The Wicker Porch

☐ **45 Turkish Chair,** white, closely woven seat and
arms, c 1900's **250.00   325.00**
Credit: The Wicker Garden

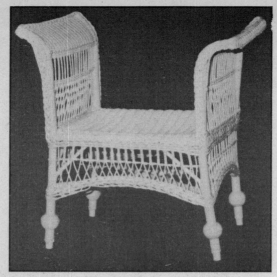

☐ **46 Turkish Chair,** white, closely woven reed seat,
ball feet, Heywood Brothers and Wakefield
Company, c 1900 .... **300.00** **400.00**
Credit: Cubbyhole Antiques

☐ **47 Turkish Chair,** white, closely woven reed seat,
curled arms, ball feet wrapped with twisted
reed, c 1910 .... **250.00** **350.00**
Credit: The Wicker Porch

COATRACKS

☐ **1 Coatrack,** white, wrapped
base, Heywood Brothers
and Wakefield Company,
c 1900's . . **200.00 295.00**
Credit: Wacky Wicker Workers

☐ **2 Coatrack,** white, wrapped
ball feet and coat hooks,
c 1910 . . . . **175.00 250.00**
Credit: The Wicker Porch

DESK

☐ **1 Desk,** white, oak top, Bar Harbor style, center drawer and side shelves for books, c 1910 . . . . .   **450.00**   **575.00**

HAMPERS

☐ **1 Hamper,** natural finish, hinged lid, closely woven reed construction, c 1910 . . . .   **75.00**   **125.00**
Credit: The Collected Works

BENCHES

☐ **1 Courting Bench,** natural finish, very rare, upholstered seats and armrest-divider, Mission style, c 1900's **500.00** **700.00**

LAMPS

☐ **1 Floor Lamp,** natural finish, "Eiffel Tower" style base, Bar Harbor design, c 1915 .... **500.00** **675.00**
Credit: Wacky Wicker Workers

☐ **2 Floor Lamp-Fernery,** white, rare, hollow reed
base, reed shade, double bulb model, c 1915 . . .   **425.00   600.00**
Credit: Arabesque Antiques

☐ **3 Table Lamp,** natural finish, large square shade is double-bulb model, unique woven globe design at center, closely woven base employs diamond design, c 1910 . . . . **275.00   375.00**
Credit: Montgomery Auction Exchange

☐ **4 Table Lamp,** white, wooden ball feet, double bulb style, silk lined shade, c 1915 . . . . **275.00   375.00**
Credit: House of Wicker

LOUNGES

☐ **1 Lounge,** natural finish, closely woven back and sides, footrest, set-in cane seat, Heywood Brothers and Company, c 1910 .... **850.00   1000.00**

☐ **2 Lounge,** natural finish, closely woven flat arms, openwork back panel, springs attached to framework, Heywood Brothers and Wakefield Company, c 1910 .... **900.00   1200.00**

☐ **3 Lounge,** white, Bar Harbor design, closely
woven seat, c 1915 . . . .   600.00   800.00
Credit: The Wicker Porch

☐ **4 Lounge,** white, Bar Harbor design, closely
woven seat, footrest and skirting, ball feet
wrapped with twisted reed, c 1910 . . . .   750.00   1000.00

☐ **5 Lounge,** white, closely woven flat back and arms, upholstered back and seat, springs attached to framework, c 1910 . . . . **725.00   1000.00**
Credit: The Collected Works

PHONOGRAPHS

☐ **1 Phonograph,** natural finish, extremely rare design, hand-crank model, double doors open to three shelf record compartment, silk lining in cabinet, fancywork includes gessoed roses, mood lamp tops this very desirable piece, c 1910 .... **1500.00 +**
Credit: Wickering Heights

☐ **2 Phonograph,** natural finish, rare table top model, Heywood Brothers and Wakefield Company, c 1918 . . . . **700.00 850.00**
Credit: Wacky Wicker Workers

☐ **3 Phonograph,** natural finish, hand-crank model, silk linedcabinet, double doors open to four shelf record storage compartment, c 1915 . . **800.00 1100.00**
Credit: Montgomery Auction Exchange

PORCH SWINGS

☐ **1 Porch Swing,** white, rare, high back Mission style, closely woven seat, wooden balls on top posts, built-in arm rests, c 1910 . . . .   **750.00   1000.00**

☐ **2 Porch Swing,** white, rare, serpentine back and arms, closely woven diamond design set into backrest and under arms, metal frame, c 1900's   **700.00   900.00**
Credit: The Collected Works

ROCKERS

☐ **1 Child's Rocker,** natural finish, lyre motif set into back, turned wood framework, Heywood Brothers and Wakefield Company, c 1900's .. **175.00 235.00**

☐ **2 Child's Rocker,** natural finish, wingback design, magazine holder on outside of left arm, closely woven seat, c 1910 .... **185.00 275.00**

Credit: Joan M. Cole Wicker

☐ **3 Child's Rocker,** white, closely woven back, arms and seat, c 1900's **165.00   220.00**
Credit: Windsor's Cane & Wicker Repair

☐ **4 Child's Rocker,** white, made of fiber, serpentine
design, turned wood frame, c 1915 . . . .   **145.00   200.00**
Credit: Wickering Heights

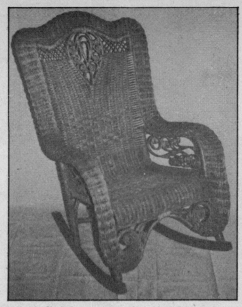

☐ **5 Rocker,** natural finish, serpentine back and arms, closely woven back and seat, c 1900's ..   **325.00   450.00**
Credit: Montgomery Auction Exchange

☐ **6 Rocker,** natural finish, serpentine back and arms, two closely woven back panels with diamond pattern, Heywood Brothers and Wakefield Company, c 1900's   **400.00   550.00**
Credit: Wacky Wicker Workers

☐ **7 Rocker,** natural finish,
serpentine back and arms,
wooden spoolwork set into
back, Larkin Chair
Company,
c 1900's .. **350.00   475.00**
Credit: The Wicker Porch

☐ **8 Rocker,** natural finish, wingback design, Paines
Furniture Company, c 1910 .... **300.00   425.00**
Credit: The Wicker Porch

☐ **9 Rocker,** white, armless variety sometimes called "sewing rockers" in turn-of-the-century
wicker trade catalogues, c 1900's **175.00   245.00**

☐ **10 Rocker,** white, basic
serpentine design, closely
woven seat, reed circles
under arms,
c 1900's . . **250.00   350.00**
Credit: The Wicker Garden

☐ **11 Rocker,** white, curled arms
end in curlicues,
c 1900's .. **300.00   435.00**
Credit: The Wicker Porch

☐ **12 Rocker,** white, flat arms, upholstered back and
seat, Heywood Brothers and Wakefield Com-
pany, c 1910 .... **275.00   375.00**

☐ **13 Rocker,** white, Mission
style, springs attached to
frame, made of thick reed,
c 1915 .... **260.00 365.00**
Credit: Wacky Wicker Workers

☐ **14 Rocker,** white, serpentine
back and arms,
c 1900's .. **300.00 425.00**
Credit: The Wicker Porch

☐ **15 Rocker,** white, serpentine back and arms, diamond design woven into fleur-de-lis back panel, closely woven skirting,
c 1900's . .   **350.00   475.00**
Credit: The Wicker Garden

☐ **16 Rocker,** white, serpentine back and arms, diamond design woven into head-rest,
c 1900's . .   **350.00   475.00**
Credit: Hidden Treasures

☐ **17 Rocker,** white, three-ply round reed used in crisscross pattern in back, c 1910 . . . . 285.00 375.00
Credit: Cubbyhole Antiques

SETS

☐ **1 Desk and Matching Chair,** natural finish, oak
top, woven side pockets for stationery, c 1915 .   **550.00   725.00**
Credit: The Collected Works

☐ **2 Desk and Matching Chair,** white, flowing design, pigeon hole divider set into back, ball feet
on both pieces, c 1900's **600.00   800.00**
Credit: The Wicker Porch

☐ **3 Dining Set,** natural finish, octagon-shaped table, oak top, chairs have set-in cane seat, c 1910 .... **1300.00 1950.00**
Credit: House of Wicker

☐ **4 Dining Set,** natural finish, round oak top, uniquely-shaped matching chairs fit snugly under table, set-in cane seats, turned wood frame, c 1910 .... **1000.00 1500.00**
Credit: Wacky Wicker Workers

☐ **5 Dining Table and Chairs,** white, matching set, oak top table, wide closely woven seats, unique shelves under seats, c 1910 .... **1400.00   1900.00**

☐ **6 Dining Table with Chairs,** white, matching set, octagon-shaped top, Mission style, c 1910 .... **1500.00   2000.00**

☐ **7 Dining Table with Chairs,** white, matching set, top is 42″ in diameter, triangular-shaped seats, extra wide backs, chairs fit into table, c 1915 .. **1000.00   1600.00**
Credit: Cubbyhole Antiques

☐ **8 Matching Armchairs and Ottoman,** natural finishes, rolled backs, closely woven design employ interesting designs set into backs, armchair at left is "gentleman's" design (slightly larger than the "ladies" design at right), ottoman has cabriole legs, c 1900s **875.00   1350.00**
Credit: A Summer Place

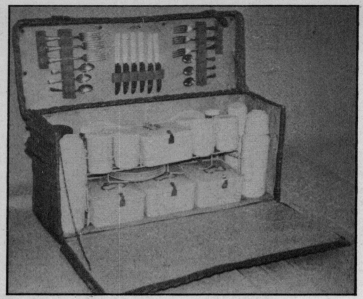

☐ **9 Tea Set,** natural finish, complete service for six, closely woven willow body, leather handles, c 1915 .... 135.00   225.00
Credit: Montgomery Auction Exchange

☐ **10 Tea Set,** natural finish, made by "Marshall Fields" of Chicago, woven of willow, c 1910 ...   125.00   185.00
Credit: Montgomery Auction Exchange

☐ **11 Tea Set,** natural finish, made by "Marshall
Fields," made of willow, made in London,
c 1910 .... **100.00   160.00**
Credit: Wickering Heights

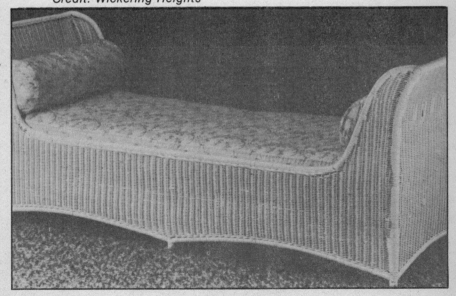

SOFAS

☐ **1 Daybed,** white, unique closely woven design,
Mission style, springs attached to framework,
possibly German-made, c 1910 .... **750.00   950.00**
Credit: The Collected Works

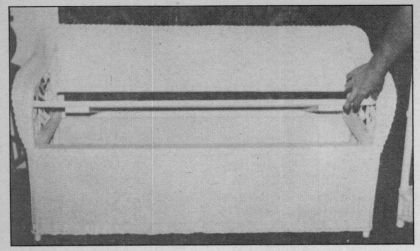

☐ 2 **Settee-Chest,** white, very rare, lift-top reveals spacious storage compartment, serpentine arms and back, closely woven bottom compartment, c 1900's .... **900.00 +**

☐ 3 **Settee,** natural finish, closely woven back and arms, rolled edges, curlicue design in lower back, c 1900's **750.00 1000.00**
Credit: A Summer Place

☐ **4 Settee,** natural finish, Mission style, closely woven seat, tall openwork side panels, ball feet, c 1910 .... 750.00 925.00
Credit: Wacky Wicker Workers

☐ **5 Settee,** natural finish, rare "one-seater" design, storage area under both half-moon shaped armrests, diamond pattern woven into back, Heywood Brothers and Wakefield Company, c 1910 800.00 1100.00
Credit: Wacky Wicker Workers

☐ **6 Settee,** natural finish, serpentine back and arms, double diamond design set into closely woven backrest, center motif employs curlicues and loops, c 1900's . . **950.00 1500.00**
Credit: The Wicker Porch

☐ **7 Settee,** natural finish, serpentine back and arms, figure eight design worked into back and skirting, ball feet wrapped with twisted reed, Heywood Brothers and Wakefield Company, c 1900's **1000.00 1500.00**
Credit: The Wicker Garden

☐ **8 Settee,** natural finish, serpentine back and arms, rosette arm tips, ball feet, closely woven back and skirting, c 1900's 625.00   800.00

Credit: The Wicker Lady

☐ **9 Settee,** natural finish, serpentine back and arms, turned wooden spools divide curlicue design in lower back, set-in cane seat, c 1900's 750.00 1000.00
Credit: Lightfoot House

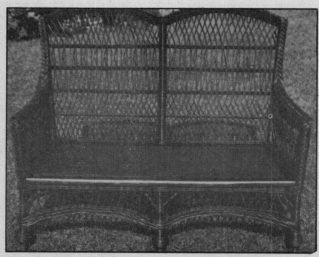

☐ **10 Settee,** natural finish, set-in cane seat, braidwork on back and arms, c 1910 . . . . 650.00 850.00
Credit: The Wicker Lady

☐ **11 Settee,** white, Bar Harbor, wingback design,
c 1910 .... **500.00   650.00**
Credit: The Wicker Porch

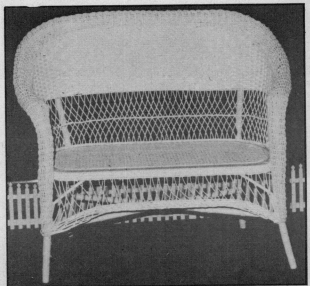

☐ **12 Settee,** white, serpentine back and arms, close-
ly woven back panel, set-in cane seat, c 1900's   **600.00   750.00**
Credit: Cubbyhole Antiques

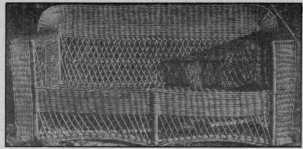

☐ **13 Sofa,** natural finish, willow, Mission style, extra long skirting, The Gustav Stickley Company, c 1910 .... 700.00   900.00
Credit: The Wicker Porch

☐ **14 Sofa,** white, Bar Harbor design, inner-spring cushions, c 1915 .... 675.00   850.00
Credit: The Wicker Lady

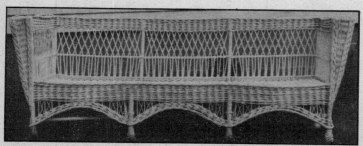

☐ **15 Sofa,** white, Mission style, ball feet wrapped with Oriental sea grass, c 1910 .... 750.00   1000.00
Credit: The Wicker Porch

STANDS

☐ **1 Fernery,** natural finish, scalloped design at center of basket, Heywood Brothers and Wakefield Company, c 1910 . . . . **150.00 225.00**
Credit: Wacky Wicker Workers

☐ **2 Night Stand,** natural finish, six-sided design, center door opens to spacious storage compartment, c 1900's . . **185.00 245.00**
Credit: Joan M. Cole Wicker

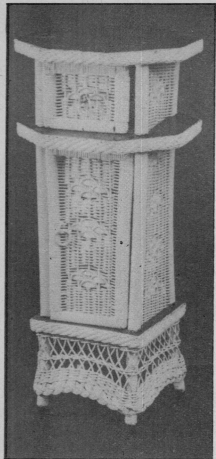

□ **3 Night Stand,** white, oak
top, top drawer pulls out,
middle door swings open,
c 1900's . . **250.00 375.00**
Credit: Heirloom Wicker

□ **4 Plant Stand,** original blue
paint, 65″ high, Bar Harbor
design, woven arch,
original reed birdcage,
metal liner,
c 1910 . . . . **450.00 600.00**

☐ **5 Plant Stand,** natural finish, oak top and framework, reed fancywork, made in Austria, c 1905 . . . .   **150.00   225.00**

☐ **6 Plant Stand,** natural finish, closely woven jardiniere-type planter with rolled edge, curlicues, ball feet, oak bottom shelf, c 1900's . .   **200.00   300.00**
Credit: Hays House of Wicker

□ **7 Plant Stand,** natural finish, hand woven of reed, wicker handles on each side, c 1910.... **175.00 250.00**
Credit: Montgomery Auction Exchange

□ **8 Plant Stand,** natural finish, willow, handles, wrapped ball feet, metal liner, c 1915 .... **140.00 170.00**
Credit: Wacky Wicker Workers

☐ **9 Plant Stand,** white, closely
woven top, Bar Harbor
design at bottom, ball feet
wrapped with twisted reed,
c 1910 . . . . **300.00   375.00**
Credit: Lightfoot House

☐ **10 Plant Stand,** white, Bar
Harbor design, reed loop
motif under planter,
c 1910 . . . . **125.00   175.00**
Credit: The Wicker Porch

☐ **11 Plant Stand,** white, closely woven design has highly unique shape, c 1910.... **250.00 350.00**
Credit: Cubbyhole Antiques

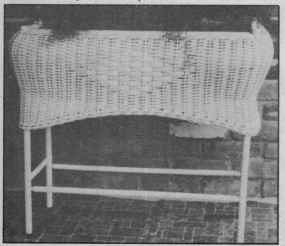

☐ **12 Plant Stand,** white, diamond pattern, turned wood frame, c 1915.... **160.00 200.00**
Credit: Wacky Wicker Workers

☐ **13 Plant Stand,** white, 72″ high, rare double planter, closely woven circular design, metal liners, made by Volmer/Prag-Rudmiker of Austria, c 1905.... **350.00 500.00**

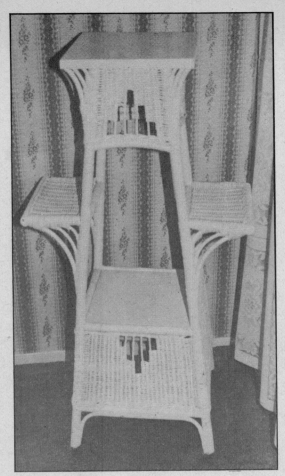

☐ **14 Plant Stand,** white, unique
design employs wooden top and
bottom shelves, two closely
woven side shelves at each side,
c 1910 . . . . **375.00   475.00**

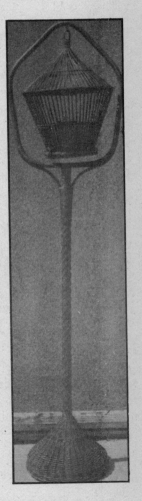

☐ **15 Standing Birdcage,**
natural finish, closely
woven base, original
cage,
c 1910   **225.00   325.00**
Credit: Hays House of Wicker

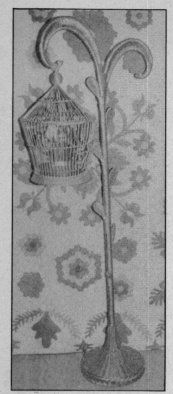

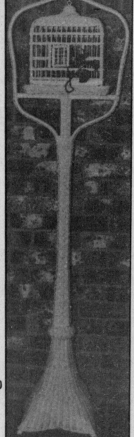

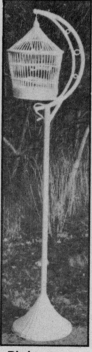

☐ **16 Standing Birdcage,**
natural finish, closely
woven leaf-shaped
sprouts and woven
base,
c 1910   350.00   450.00
Credit: A Summer Place

☐ **17 Standing Birdcage,**
white, elaborate design,
closely woven skirting,
c 1900's   350.00   425.00

☐ **18 Standing Birdcage,**
white, crescent moon
arch is very popular, all
reed construction,
c 1900's   235.00   325.00

STOOLS

☐ **1 Footstool,** white, 16″ x 24″, caned top, c 1900's . .   **135.00**   **185.00**
Credit: The Wicker Garden

☐ **2 Ottoman,** natural finish, closely woven design, velvet upholstery not original, c 1900's . .   **125.00**   **175.00**
Credit: Montgomery Auction Exchange

☐ **3 Ottoman,** white, closely woven top, ball feet wrapped with twisted reed, circular flower design on sides, c 1900's . .   **125.00**   **200.00**
Credit: The Wicker Porch

☐ **4 Taboret,** natural finish, 20″
high, oak top, six turned
wood legs,
c 1910 .... **175.00   250.00**
Credit: The Wicker Garden

☐ **5 Taboret,** white, 21″ high,
curved legs, The Gustav
Stickley Company,
c 1905 .... **175.00   225.00**
Credit: The Wicker Porch

STROLLERS

☐ **1 Baby Stroller,** white, closely woven diamond design, adjustable hood, sometimes called "Go-Carts" in turn-of-the-century wicker trade catalogues, c 1915 . . . . **450.00   650.00**

☐ **2 Stroller,** natural finish,
Heywood Brothers and
Wakefield Company,
flowing design incor-
porates curlicues and
closely woven reedwork,
rubber tires,
c 1900's .. **325.00   450.00**
*Credit: Montgomery Auction
Exchange*

☐ **3 Stroller,** natural finish, fold-up style, unique
woven side pockets, c 1910 .... **300.00   400.00**
Credit: Wacky Wicker Workers

☐ **4 Stroller,** natural finish, fold-up style, star design
woven into sides, rubber tires, c 1910 . . . .   380.00   550.00
Credit: Wacky Wicker Workers

TABLES

☐ **1 Dining Table,** white, oak top is 42″ in diameter, woven design on legs and braces, ball feet, c 1910 .... **600.00   775.00**
Credit: The Wicker Porch

☐ **2 End Table,** natural finish, half-moon top, rustic "stick" design, diamond pattern created by crisscross Oriental sea grass weave, c 1910 ... **120.00   165.00**
Credit: Isgrow & Company

☐ **3 End Table,** natural finish, square oak top, closely woven base, oak bottom shelf, wooden ball
feet, Heywood Brothers and Wakefield Com-
pany, c 1900's **225.00   320.00**
Credit: Wacky Wicker Workers

☐ **4 Hutch Table,** natural finish, extremely rare design in wicker which was adapted from the "settle" chair of Pilgrim origin, closely woven table top lifts to form an armchair, pine frame, c 1915 .... **375.00 500.00**
Credit: Jean Newhart's Antiques

☐ **5 Library Table,** natural finish, rare design employs center drawer, oak top and shelves, side sections for books, c 1910 .... 500.00   650.00
Credit: The Wicker Garden

☐ **6 Oblong Table,** natural finish, oak top and bottom shelf, some fancywork on skirting, c 1900's   275.00   375.00
Credit: Montgomery Auction Exchange

☐ **7 Oblong Table,** white, odd mixture of reed, cane, rush, Oriental sea grass, willow and rattan, ball feet have small metal casters, c 1910 . . . .   **275.00   375.00**

☐ **8 Oval Table,** white, Bar Harbor design, unique magazine pockets on inside of bottom shelf, c 1910 . . . .   **300.00   400.00**
Credit: The Wicker Porch

☐ **9 Oval Table,** white, serpentine edges, closely woven skirting, small oval bottom shelf, ball feet,
c 1900's **300.00 375.00**
Credit: The Wicker Porch

☐ **10 Round Table,** white, Bar Harbor design, circular woven top and bottom shelf employs wooden center piece,
c 1910 . **225.00 300.00**
Credit: The Wicker Porch

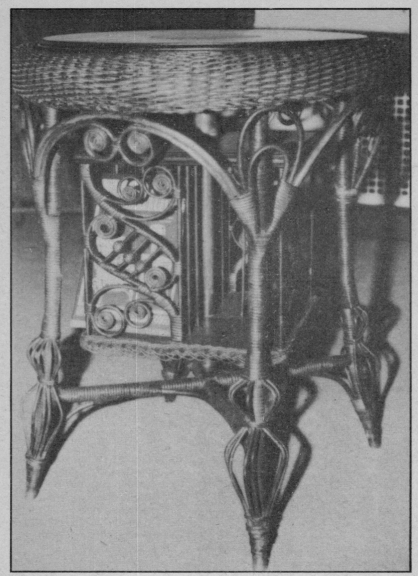

☐ **11 Round Table,** natural finish, very rare, revolving
bookcase on bottom shelf, birdcage legs, Heywood Brothers and Wakefield Company,
c 1900's 700.00   900.00
Credit: A Summer Place

☐ **12 Round Table,** white, glass top, "elephant trunk"
legs, square bottom shelf, Heywood Brothers
and Wakefield Company, c 1900's **325.00   450.00**
Credit: Cubbyhole Antiques

☐ **13 Round Table,** white, oak
top and bottom shelf,
Niagra Reed Company,
c 1910 . . . . **250.00   350.00**
*Credit: Windsor's Cane & Wicker
Repair*

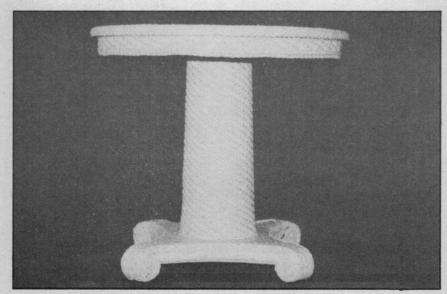

☐ **14 Round Table,** white, rare Empire style, closely
woven pedestal and curled legs, c 1910 . . . . **650.00   850.00**
Credit: The Wicker Porch

☐ **15 Round Table,** white, serpentine edges, closely woven top and bottom shelf, c 1910 . . . **225.00 325.00**

☐ **16 Serving Table,** white, rare, willow, lift-off glass tray, thick braidwork, c 1915 . . . . **250.00 375.00**
Credit: Wacky Wicker Workers

☐ **17 Side Table,** natural finish, 18″ in diameter, oak top, serpentine edges, fancy-work on round bottom shelf, turned wood legs, c 1900's .. **275.00   375.00**

☐ **18 Square Table,** white, closely woven top, ball design at top of legs wrapped with Oriental sea grass, round bottom shelf, c 1910 . . . .   **300.00   400.00**

☐ **19 Square Table,** white, oak top and bottom shelf,
ball feet, c 1900's **265.00   385.00**

☐ **20 Square Table,** white,
twisted reed wrapped
around feet,
c 1910 . . . .   **175.00   245.00**

□ **21 Table,** natural finish, 36″ long, oak top, ball feet, c 1910 . . . . **200.00** **300.00**
Credit: Montgomery Auction Exchange

□ **22 Table,** natural finish, square oak top is finished off with closely woven skirting, bottom shelf is enclosed by square woven panels, c 1910 . . . . **275.00** **350.00**
Credit: Montgomery Auction Exchange

TEA CARTS

☐ **1 Tea Cart,** natural finish, closely woven covered utensil basket, lift-off glass tray, bottom shelf, two ball feet in rear, c 1910 . . . .   **425.00   550.00**
Credit: Joan M. Cole Wicker

☐ **2 Tea Cart,** natural finish, lift-off tray, three shelves, wooden wheels, c 1910 . . . .   **475.00   600.00**
Credit: The Wicker Garden

☐ **3 Tea Cart,** natural finish, rare storage area under tray, wooden wheels with brass fittings, Heywood Brothers and Wakefield Company, c 1910   **500.00**   **650.00**
Credit: Cubbyhole Antiques

☐ **4 Tea Cart,** white, unique flowing design, wooden wheels, lift-off tray, closely woven bottom shelf, c 1905 . . . . **400.00 550.00**
Credit: Hays House of Wicker

MISCELLANEOUS

☐ **1 Blanket Chest,** natural finish, woven diamond design on front and sides, closely woven reed, ball feet, rare design used at the foot of the bed for easy access to blankets, c 1900's **450.00 550.00**
Credit: A Summer Place

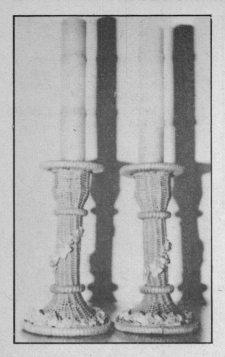

☐ **2 Candle Holders,** very rare, natural finish, 7″ high, gessoed roses, intricately woven wickerwork, c 1910 .... **100.00   225.00**
Credit: A Summer Place

☐ **3 Doll Bed,** white, very rare, 20″ x 23″, ball feet, c 1900's **200.00   300.00**

☐ **4 Dressing Screen,** white, three closely woven
panels, ornate design set into circular motif at
top of each panel, c 1910 . . . . **400.00   550.00**
Credit: Joan M. Cole Wicker

☐ **5 Frames,** natural finish, rare matching pair, Oriental sea grass woven around photos and
glass, for the pair, c 1915 . . . . **150.00   235.00**
Credit: The Collected Works

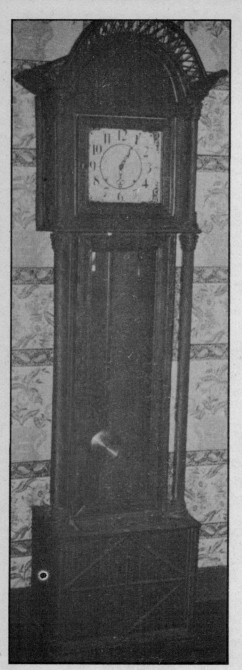

☐ **6 Grandfather's Clock,**
natural finish, rare,
closely woven reed mat-
ting on cabinet, original
clock face, arched top
employs crisscross
design,
c 1910 . **1500.00** +
Credit: Hays House of Wicker

☐ **7 Halltree,** natural finish, very rare, sunburst motif in back panel and under arms, large beveled mirror, brass hooks, made of Oriental sea grass, rush, reed and cane, c 1900's . . . . . . **1350.00 +**
Credit: Hays House of Wicker

☐ **8 Long Seat,** white, rare, Mission style, ball feet
and corner posts are wrapped with twisted willow, c 1910 .... 400.00   500.00
Credit: The Wicker Lady

☐ **9 Magazine Rack,** natural
finish, Oriental sea
grass, rustic framework,
three legs,
c 1910 . 145.00   195.00
Credit: Hays House of Wicker

☐ **10 Pie Caddy,** white, three-tier design, circular
woven reed shelves, c 1900's **125.00**   **175.00**
Credit: Windsor's Cane & Wicker Repair

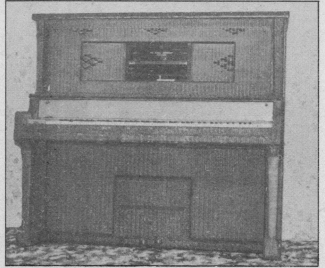

☐ **11 Player Piano, Bench and Matching Piano Roll Cabinet,** extremely rare set, natural brown stain with diamond design painted orange and black at the factory, a custom made piece which is very possibly one-of-a-kind, panels above the keyboard open to reveal piano rolls, cabinet made by the Stuyvesant Piano Company of New York City, manufacturer of the wickerwork covering is unknown, c 1906 .... **5000.00 +**
Credit: Carnes/Gibson, Private

☐ **12 Pony Cart,** natural finish, rare, made of willow, large wooden wheels, c 1910 .... **275.00   375.00**
Credit: Cubbyhole Antiques

☐ **13 Tantalus,** natural finish, extremely rare, closely woven reed and Oriental sea grass, Lambeth Doulton Stoneware jugs marked "G" for Gin, "SW" for Scotch Whiskey and "IW" for Irish Whiskey, c 1905 .... **250.00 +**
Credit: The Collected Works

☐ **14 Vanity,** natural finish, very rare, beveled mirror, woven matting covers drawer and cabinet, Heywood Brothers and Wakefield Company, c 1900's .... **1500.00 +**
Credit: The Wicker Porch

☐ **15 Velocipede,** natural finish, extremely rare, serpentine back and arms, diamond design woven into backrest, rubber tires, metal label reads "Fairy," made by the Colson Chair Company of Elyria, Ohio, c 1900's . . . . **750.00 +**
Credit: The Wicker Garden

☐ **16 Wheelchair,** natural finish, rare, serpentine
back and arms, set-in cane seat and leg rest,
rubber tires, c 1900's 350.00   600.00
Credit: Lightfoot House

WICKER FURNITURE OF THE 1920s

In the 1920s economic factors (rather than a public shift in taste) determined what type of wicker furniture would be on the market. While inexpensive open-weave latticework "Bar Harbor" styles were the rage since 1905, the popularity of closely woven wicker was finally met by the introduction of the Lloyd loom. Invented by Marshall B. Lloyd in 1917, this machine wove sheets of a relatively new man-made material called "fiber" (a chemically-treated twisted paper) which was, in turn, fitted over simple frames which were attuned to functionalism and the lessons of mass production.

Beyond mere economic factors the "Art Deco" style (which believed in rational construction, balance of line and general harmony of design) had taken hold by the mid-1920s. Readily accepting the role of the machine and mass production, the Art Deco style and the Lloyd loom seemed like a "natural" for wicker furniture. However, as the years passed by it became increasingly evident that the public was growing dissatisfied with machine-made wicker. The strongest link between wicker furniture and the American consumer had always been the fact that it was completely handmade. Now, somehow, it seemed to lose its individuality and character. Finally, toward the end of the 1920s the public revolted against the growing lack of true craftsmanship and the early 1930s witnessed the death of what was once a giant American industry.

BASKETS

☐ **1 Child's Sewing Basket,** white, hinged lid, closely woven basket and bottom shelf, c 1920's . . **120.00 175.00**
Credit: Heirloom Wicker

☐ **2 Sewing Basket,** white, willow, circular top and bottom baskets, ball feet, stationary handle, c 1920's . . **125.00 175.00**
Credit: Wacky Wicker Workers

☐ **3 Sewing Basket,** white,
wrapped circular handles,
turned wood framework,
ball feet,
c 1925 ... **125.00 160.00**
Credit: The Wicker Porch

☐ **4 Wood Basket,** white, diamond design woven into both sides, c 1920's **75.00 100.00**

BASSINETS

☐ **1 Bassinet on Wheels,** white, folding hood, wooden wheels, rubber tires, c 1925 . . . . **225.00 325.00**
Credit: The Collected Works

☐ **2 Bassinet,** white, willow, openwork hood, ball feet on casters, c 1920's . . **200.00 285.00**
Credit: Wacky Wicker Workers

BUFFET

☐ **1 Buffet,** white, two drawers, closely woven back and sides, c 1925 .... **700.00   850.00**
Credit: The Collected Works

☐ **2 Buffet/Server,** white, rare, four glass-panel cupboards, three silverware drawers, wicker inserts in bottom cupboard doors, woven top and sides, Highpoint Bending and Chair Company, c 1920's .. **2000.00 +**
Credit: A Summer Place

CHAIRS

☐ **1 Armchair,** natural finish, multi-colored "French enameled" cane, c. 1920's . **150.00 200.00**
Credit: Montgomery Auction Exchange

☐ **2 Armchair,** white, closely woven arms of flat reed, inner-spring cushion, padded back rest, c 1925 . . . . **200.00 300.00**
Credit: Allen's Antiques

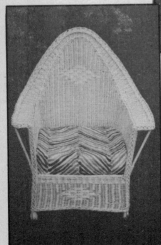

☐ **3 Armchair,** white, cathedral-back design, diamond pattern woven into back and under seat, hundreds of reed, inner-spring cushion, ball feet, c 1920's . . **285.00 385.00**
Credit: The Wicker Lady

□ **4 Armchair,** white, closely
woven design, retractable
foot rest, woven roll in
lower back for extra com-
fort,
c 1920's . . **375.00 475.00**
Credit: The Wicker Lady

□ **5 Armchair,** white, handmade
of fiber, diamond design
set into backrest,
c 1920's . . **235.00 325.00**
Credit: Arabesque Antiques

□ **7 Armchair,** white, handmade
of fiber, upholstered
backrest, inner-spring
cushion,
c 1920's . . **235.00 300.00**
Credit: Wacky Wicker Workers

□ **6 Armchair,** white, handmade
of fiber, upholstered
backrest and cushion,
c 1920's . . **235.00 335.00**

☐ **8 Armchair,** white, handmade of reed, diamond design woven into back and sides, rare decorative wickerwork under arm rests, inner-spring cushion, c 1920's **350.00** **465.00**
Credit: The Wicker Garden

☐ **9 Armchair,** white, heavy inner-spring cushion, made of fiber, c 1920's .. **220.00** **275.00**

☐ **10 Armchair,** white, made of
fiber, inner-spring cushion,
c 1920 . . . **285.00   350.00**

☐ **11 Armchair,** white, reed
openwork in backrest,
inner-spring cushion, ball
feet wrapped with reed,
c 1920's . . **300.00   375.00** '

☐ **12 Armchair,** white, unique
closely woven gentleman's
armchair is handmade of
reed, diamond design
woven into backrest,
c 1920's . . **350.00   425.00**

☐ **13 Armchair,** white, closely woven design, diamond pattern woven into back, c. 1920's **250.00**   **325.00**
Credit: Montgomery Auction Exchange

☐ **14 Child's Armchair,** white,
made of Oriental sea grass
and reed trim,
c 1920's . .   **140.00** **180.00**

☐ **15 Doll's High Chair,** white, rare, 27″ high, pine
frame, closely woven reed backrest, tray and
footrest, c 1925 .... **150.00   200.00**

☐ **16 Side Chair,** natural finish,
multi-colored "French
enameled" cane,
c 1920's ...   **90.00   145.00**
*Credit: Montgomery Auction
Exchange*

☐ **17 Side Chair,** natural finish,
handmade of reed, diamond
woven into back, openwork
skirting, loop motif in top of
backrest,
c 1920's ...   **125.00   175.00**

☐ **18 Side Chair,** natural finisn,
made of reed, closely woven
seat,
c 1920's ...   **100.00   145.00**
Credit: The Wicker Porch

☐ **19 Side Chair,** natural finish,
unique braided construction,
of handmade fiber,
c 1920's ...   **90.00   135.00**
Credit: Wisteria Antiques

☐ **20 Side Chair,** white, machine-made of fiber by the Lloyd loom, turned wood legs, ball feet on front legs, Heywood-Wakefield Company, c 1920's ...   **90.00   125.00**
Credit: The Wicker Garden

☐ **21 Side Chair,** white, made of fiber, back panel employs wire-centered fiber for added strength, c 1920's ...   **95.00   135.00**

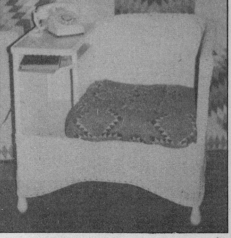

☐ **22 Side Chair,** white, made of fiber, crisscross design in backrest employs wire centered fiber for added strength, c 1920's ...   **115.00   145.00**

☐ **23 Telephone Chair,** rare, close-ly woven reed design, oak side shelf holds telephone, shelf below is designed for telephone book, c 1920's ...   **500.00   650.00**
Credit: A Summer Place

COAT RACKS

☐ **1 Child's Coat Rack,** white, rare, 28″ high, closely woven base, gessoed roses on base and pole, wooden hooks, c 1920's . . **150.00 235.00**

☐ **2 Coat Rack,** white, closely woven design, metal hooks, diamond design at base, intricately woven dome at top, c 1920's . . **285.00 370.00**

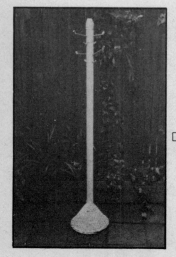

☐ **3 Coat Rack,** white, twisted reed center post, metal hooks, c 1920's . . **200.00 275.00**

DAYBED

☐ **1 Daybed,** white, closely woven reed, diamond
design, inner-spring mattress, c 1920's **650.00**   **850.00**

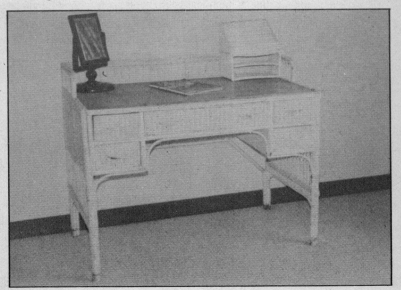

DESKS

☐ **1 Desk,** white, five drawers, closely woven design
handmade of reed, c 1920s **400.00**   **550.00**

☐ **2 Desk,** white, oak top, wide drawer with brass
pulls, letter holders on sides, c. 1920's 300.00   450.00

☐ **3 Office Desk,** white, rare, eight legs, five
drawers, bottom storage shelves, diamond
design woven into back and sides, c 1920's 800.00   1100.00
Credit: The Collected Works

☐ **4 Rolltop Secretary,** natural finish, extremely rare, diamond designs are stained in muted green tones, two glass doors, cylinderical roll-top opens to desk, intricate cathedral kneehole design, possibly a custom-made piece, the manufacturer is unknown, c 1920's . . . . **3500.00 +**

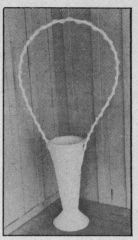

FERNERY

☐ **1 Fernery,** natural finish, handmade of fiber, 48″ tall,
c 1920s . . . **150.00 225.00**
Credit: Wacky Wicker Workers

☐ **2 Fernery,** white, 5 feet tall, cone-shaped metal liner, closely woven base made of reed,
c 1920's . . **85.00 160.00**
Credit: Arabesque Antiques

☐ **3 Fernery,** white, unique design employs closely woven handles,
c 1920's . . **150.00 225.00**
Credit: Hays House of Wicker

☐ **4 Fernery,** white, cane-wrapped arch for hanging birdcage,
c 1920's . . **350.00 450.00**

☐ **5 Fernery,** white, closely
woven style employs dia-
mond design woven into
basket, rolled lip,
c 1920's .. **145.00   225.00**
*Credit: Montgomery Auction
Exchange*

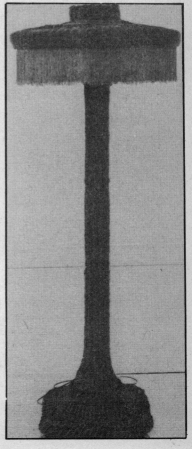

LAMPS

☐ **1 Floor Lamp,** natural finish,
fringe hangs from closely
woven shade,
c 1920's .. **350.00   475.00**
Credit: Wacky Wicker Workers

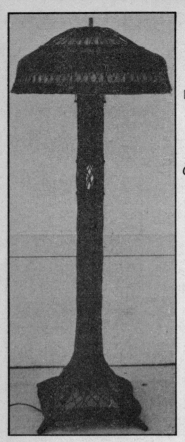

☐ **2 Floor Lamp,** natural finish, 6' tall, silk lined shade, double bulb model, Heywood-Wakefield Company, c 1920's .. **350.00 450.00**
Credit: Wacky Wicker Workers

☐ **3 Floor Lamp,** white "Eiffel Tower" design, unique braidwork adorns neck, c 1920's .. **450.00 600.00**

☐ **4 Floor Lamp,** white, made
   of finely-woven fiber,
   unique shade,
   c 1920's . . **350.00 450.00**
Credit: A Summer Place

☐ **5 Floor Lamp,** white, unique
   pagoda-shaped shade,
   c 1920's . . **325.00 425.00**
Credit: The Collected Works

☐ **6 Table Lamp,** natural finish,
rare, unique use of multi-
colored glass beaded
fringe under shade, rarely
seen hand-painted wooden
section above base,
c 1920's . . **325.00 400.00**
Credit: Hays House of Wicker

☐ **7 Table Lamp,** natural finish,
dark-stained reeds form a
circular design on base,
brass finial,
c 1920's . . **200.00 300.00**
Credit: Hays House of Wicker

☐ **8 Table Lamp,** natural finish,
thick loop design on
shade, closely woven base,
c 1920's . . **275.00 340.00**
Credit: Wacky Wicker Workers

☐ **9 Table Lamp,** natural finish,
under shade,
c 1920's .. **225.00 320.00**
Credit: Wacky Wicker Workers

☐ **10 Table Lamp,** natural finish,
unique in that it lacks a
wooden base, woven reed
frame,
c 1920's .. **225.00 300.00**
Credit: Wacky Wicker Workers

☐ **11 Table Lamp,** natural finish,
single bulb model, silk-
lined shade,
c 1920's .. **200.00 300.00**
*Credit: Montgomery Auction
Exchange*

☐ **12 Table Lamp,** white, machine-made of fiber by the Lloyd loom, uniformly webbed wickerwork is fitted over wood frame, Heywood-Wakefield Company, c 1920's .. **185.00 285.00**

☐ **13 Table Lamp,** white, intricate wickerwork on base and neck, brass finial, c 1920's .. **260.00 350.00**

☐ **14 Table Lamp,** white, made of willow, closely woven base, brass finial, c 1920's .. **200.00 275.00**
Credit: Wacky Wicker Workers

☐ **15 Table Lamp,** white, made
of fiber, single bulb model,
c 1920's .. **165.00 235.00**
Credit: Wacky Wicker Workers

☐ **16 Table Lamp,** white, rare,
made by hand with
Oriental sea grass, Art
Deco shade is woven sea
grass over wire framework,
double built model,
c 1925 .... **275.00 350.00**

☐ **17 Table Lamp,** white, rare,
unique porcelain frog for
flower arrangements,
shade is Bar Harbor
design,
c 1920's .. **260.00 360.00**
Credit: Hays House of Wicker

LOUNGES

☐ **1 Child's Lounge,** painted brown, rare, made of
fiber, Bar Harbor design, c 1920's **325.00   450.00**

☐ **2 Lounge,** natural finish, willow, unique one-arm
design, ball feet, c 1920's **700.00   850.00**
Credit: Bale Mill Inn & Antiques

☐ **3 Lounge,** white, Bar Harbor, design, closely woven arms and seat, c 1920's . . **800.00 1000.00**

☐ **4 Lounge,** white, Bar Harbor design, inner-spring mattress, handmade of reed, c 1920's **775.00 1000.00**
Credit: Arabesque Antiques

☐ **5 Lounge,** white, made of fiber, diamond design
woven into back, upholstered, c 1920's **800.00   950.00**
Credit: Isgrow & Company

☐ **6 Lounge,** white, Mission style, open-weave back,
closely woven seat, ball feet, handmade of
reed, c 1920's **750.00   875.00**
Credit: Cubbyhole Antiques

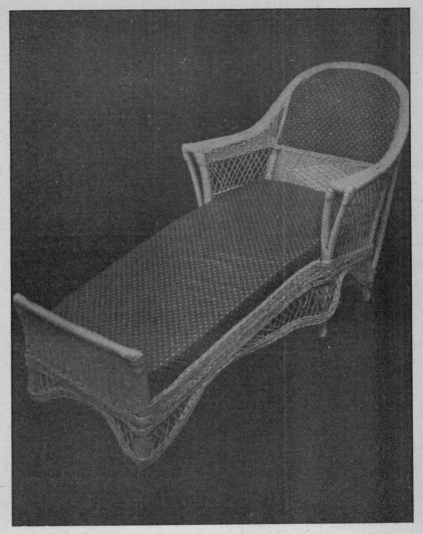

☐ **7 Lounge,** white, upholstered back and seat, closely woven fiber design, footrest, diamond design woven into lower back, openwork on skirting, c 1920's **775.00   950.00**
Credit: The Collected Works

RADIOS

☐ **1 Standing Radio,** natural finish, extremely rare, graceful flowing design, unit also includes a wicker speaker not shown (now being restored after severe fire damage), including speaker, c 1920's .... **1750.00 +**
Credit: Hays House of Wicker

☐ **2 Radio with Wicker Speaker,** natural finish, extremely rare, table model, R.C.A.'s first electric radio (R.C.A. Radiola 18″), metal speaker is covered with openwork reed design, closely woven base, c 1920's **.000.00 +**
Credit: A Summer Place

ROCKERS

☐ **1 Child's Rocker,** painted green, 24″ high, upholstered seat, springs attached to frame, c 1920's .. **115.00 150.00**
Credit: The Wicker Porch

☐ **2 Child's Rocker,** white, Bar Harbor design, c 1920's .. **135.00 180.00**

☐ **3 Rocker,** natural finish, Bar Harbor, box spring cushion and high quality upholstery job, Heywood-Wakefield Company, c 1920's .. **275.00 375.00**
Credit: Wisteria Antiques

□ **4 Rocker,** natural finish, upholstery covers inner-spring seat and cotton-filled backrest, fiber wickerwork is machine woven, c 1920's . . **175.00 250.00**

□ **5 Rocker,** painted back and brown, diamond design woven into back and under seat, fancy braidwork covers framework, made of fiber, c 1920's . . **200.00 290.00**
Credit: Bale Mill Inn & Antiques

□ **6 Rocker,** white, Bar Harbor design made of thick reed, springs attached to frame, c 1920's . . **200.00 300.00**

☐ **7 Rocker,** white, closely woven fiber design is made by hand, c 1920's .. **225.00   285.00**

☐ **8 Rocker,** white, made of fiber, crisscross pieces and skirting are reinforced by wire-centered fiber, c 1920's .. **250.00   360.00**

☐ **9 Rocker,** white, made of fiber, quality upholstery job covers backrest and seat, c 1920's .. **250.00   350.00**

☐ **10 Rocker,** white, original tie-on back pad and seat cushion are recovered, hand-woven reed seat under cushion, c 1920's .. **225.00   325.00**
Credit: The Collected Works

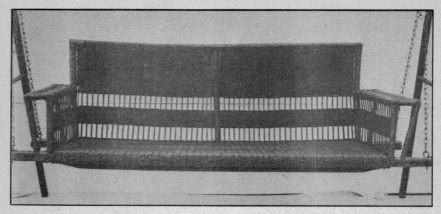

PORCH SWINGS

☐ **1 Porch Swing,** natural finish, includes "free standing" metal arches, machine-made fiber, c 1920's **750.00 1000.00**
Credit: Wacky Wicker Workers

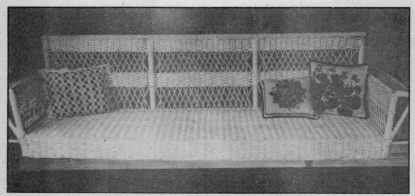

☐ **2 Porch Swing,** white, rare, 7' long, metal framework under seat, made of fiber, c 1920's **700.00 950.00**

☐ **3 Porch Swing,** white, rare, wickerwork is machine-made with fiber, 4' long, metal framework under seat, c 1920's **485.00 600.00**

SETS

☐ **1 Card Table and Four Chairs,** natural finish, rare, unique set employs four side panels under top for cards or drinks, oak octagon top, four matching low-back chairs,
c 1920's **1500.00 2000.00**
Credit: A Summer Place

☐ **2 Chest of Drawers and Layette,** white, gessoed, roses on both pieces, glass drawer pulls, c 1920's ....

    Chest of Drawers **200.00 275.00**

    Layette **500.00 700.00**

Credit: A Summer Place

☐ **3 Desk and Chair,** natural finish, matching set, oak top and drawer, woven stationery holders on desk top, c 1920's .. **600.00 750.00**

Credit: Wacky Wicker Workers

☐ **4 Desk Set,** natural finish, handmade of fiber, desk employs woven stationery holder, one center drawer, c 1920's . . **500.00   750.00**
Credit: Montgomery Auction Exchange

☐ **5 Desk Set,** white, oak top and drawer, two closely woven letter holders, Brighton Furniture Company, c 1920's **450.00   600.00**
Credit: Wacky Wicker Workers

☐ **6 Desk Set,** white, single drawer, machine made
on the Lloyd Loom, wooden top, three separate
letter holders, c 1920's 500.00   675.00

☐ **7 Dining Set,** white, eight matching chairs,
c 1920's 2250.00   2850.00

Credit: The Collected Works

☐ **8 Four Piece Set,** white, made of fiber, unupholstered lounge, upholstered settee, armchair and matching ottoman, springs attached to frame, c 1920's 1400.00   1700.00
Credit: Wacky Wicker Workers

☐ **9 Four Piece Set,** white, rare, unupholstered, Art Deco style, bookshelves built into back of sofa arms, c. 1925 . . . .   1500.00 +
Credit: Wickering Heights

☐ **10 Telephone Table and Chair,** natural finish, rare, Bar Harbor design, top shelf for phone book, low backed matching chair, c 1920's 300.00   450.00
Credit: The Wicker Porch

☐ **11 Three Piece Set,** white, sofa, armchair and rocker, closely woven backs, inner-spring cushions, c 1920's 1350.00 1750.00
Credit: The Collected Works

☐ **12 Three Piece Set,** white, two side chairs and small round table with bottom shelf, c 1920's . . 350.00 550.00
Credit: The Wicker Lady

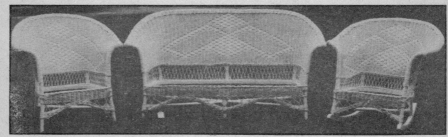

☐ **13 Three Piece Set,** white, unupholstered, made of
fiber, unique design woven into back, c 1920's . . **1400.00 1850.00**
Credit: The Wicker Lady

☐ **14 Three Piece Set,** white, unupholstered sofa,
springs attached to frame, c 1920's **900.00 1400.00**
Credit: Wickering Heights

☐ **15 Vanity and Matching Chair,** white, closely woven oval shaped desk, c 1920's **550.00** **675.00**
Credit: Cubbyhole Antiques

SOFAS

☐ **1 Child's Settee,** white, closely woven Oriental sea grass, c 1920's **200.00** **350.00**

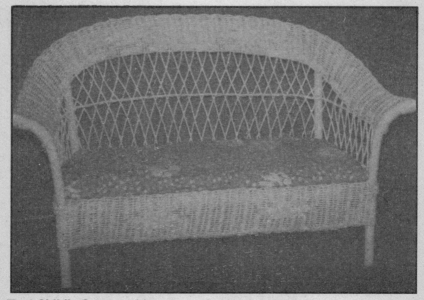

☐ **2 Child's Settee,** white, rare salesman's sample, made of fiber, Bar Harbor design, c 1920's **375.00** **500.00**

☐ **3 Settee,** white, Bar Harbor design, closely woven, reed seat, ball legs, wrapped with twisted reed, c 1920's **500.00**   **700.00**
Credit: Cubbyhole Antiques

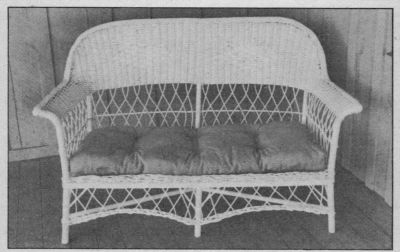

☐ **4 Settee,** white, handmade of fiber, closely woven back and arms, diamond designs in back, c 1920's **550.00**   **685.00**
Credit: Arabesque Antiques

☐ **5 Sofa,** white, closely woven design, horizontally woven reed seat, diamond patterns woven into back, c 1920's **500.00   700.00**
Credit: Montgomery Auction Exchange

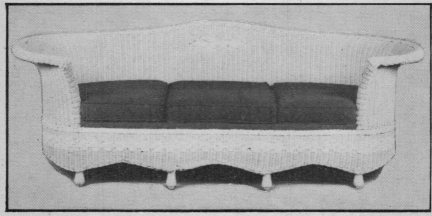

☐ **6 Sofa,** white, closely woven reed design, unique curving arms turn inwards at ends, c 1920's . . . **675.00   850.00**
Credit: Montgomery Auction Exchange

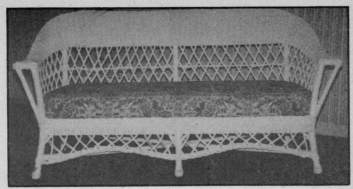

☐ **7 Sofa,** white, inner-spring mattress, ball feet, made of fiber, c 1920's **500.00** **750.00**

☐ **8 Sofa,** white, made of fiber, upholstered back and three-cushioned seat, c 1920's **550.00** **750.00**
Credit: Wacky Wicker Workers

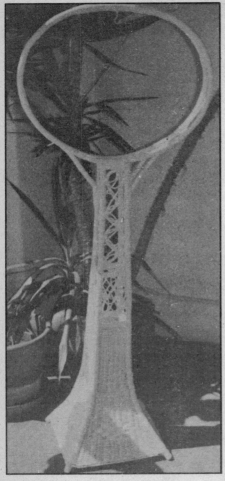

STANDS

☐ **1 Birdcage Stand,** white,
closely woven base,
circular arch,
c 1920's . . **250.00 350.00**
Credit: Lightfoot House

☐ **2 Birdcage Stand,** white,
crescent moon design,
closely woven reed,
c 1920's . . **175.00 250.00**
Credit: The Wicker Lady

☐ **3 Birdcage Stand and Birdcage,** white, closely woven
base, wrapped metal arch,
willow birdcage,
c 1920's .. **300.00 385.00**

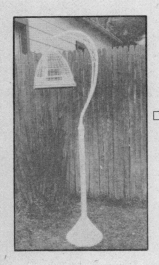

☐ **4 Birdcage Stand and Birdcage,** white, crescent
moonshaped arch,
c 1920's .. **275.00 375.00**

☐ **5 Cake Stand and Cover,**
natural finish, handmade
of reed, openwork design
tells us that it is a decorative rather than prac-
tical piece for a cake
would dry out if left in it
for any length of time,
c 1920's .. **100.00 160.00**
Credit: The Collected Works

☐ **8 Fernery-Umbrella Stand,**
white, very rare, 7′ tall,
c 1920's . . **550.00 725.00**

☐ **6 Coat Rack-Umbrella Stand,**
white, bentwood hooks,
wrapped center post, fiber,
c 1920's . . **250.00 350.00**
Credit: The Collected Works

☐ **7 Pipe Stand,** white, very
rare, oval oak top has four
holes for pipes, bottom
shelf for tobacco canister,
Bar Harbor design,
c 1920's . . **175.00 250.00**
Credit: The Collected Works

☐ **9 Plant Stand,** natural finish, extensive turned
wood framework, scalloped reedwork, c 1920's   140.00   185.00
Credit: The Wicker Lady

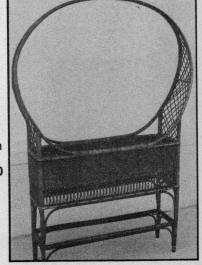

☐ **10 Plant Stand,** natural finish,
open weave in side of circular arch, diamond design
in center, metal liner,
c 1920's ..   **450.00   575.00**
Credit: Wacky Wicker Workers

☐ **11 Plant Stand,** natural finish, 46″ long, square
bottom shelf, c 1920's **145.00   200.00**

☐ **12 Plant Stand,** natural finish, rare, double planters on each side, aquarium in the center, reed
birdcage hangs from 5 foot tall arch, c 1920's . .   **550.00   775.00**
Credit: A Summer Place

☐ **13 Plant Stand,** white, Bar
Harbor design coupled
with closely woven
wickerwork,
c 1920's . . **150.00 200.00**
Credit: Lightfoot House

☐ **14 Plant Stand,** white, closely woven design, scalloped reedwork, turned wood frame, c 1920's . . **135.00 180.00**
Credit: The Wicker Garden

□ **15 Plant Stand,** white, machine-made of fiber, turned wood legs, wooden bottom shelf, c 1920's . . **115.00 145.00**
Credit: The Wicker Garden

□ **16 Plant Stand,** white, machine-made on the Lloyd
Loom, turned wood framework, c 1920's **175.00 235.00**

☐ **17 Plant Stand,** white, rare, double planters at left and right, hanging birdcage on 6 foot arch, center section for aquarium, diamond design in planter sections, c 1920's 550.00   750.00
Credit: Joan M. Cole Wicker

☐ **18 Plant Stand,** white, square design, turned wood framework, handmade of fibers, c 1920's . .   100.00   135.00
Credit: The Wicker Lady

☐ **19 Punch Bowl,** standing, natural finish, extremely rare, 32″ high, serpentine sections for glasses, metal outer canister for punch, center canister for ice, c 1920's .. **375.00   500.00**

☐ **20 Punch Server,** natural finish, table-top design, circular center for punch bowl, sectioned outer circle divided to keep glasses from tipping, twisted reed handle, c 1920's **150.00   200.00**
Credit: Montgomery Auction Exchange

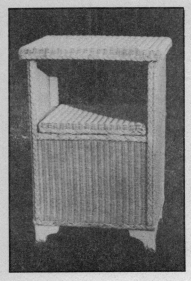

☐ **21 Night Stand,** rare, white, bottom shelf serves as a lift-top for the built-in hamper, closely woven fiber is machine-made, c 1920's .. **140.00 185.00**
Credit: The Wicker Porch

☐ **22 Night Stand,** white, square oak top and three painted shelves, handmade of fiber, c 1920's .. **185.00 250.00**
Credit: Wacky Wicker Workers

☐ **23 Smoking Stand,** white,
bottom shelf,
c 1920's . . **100.00 130.00**
Credit: The Wicker Porch

☐ **24 Smoking Stand,** white,
arched handle, made of
fiber,
c 1920's . . **125.00 165.00**
Credit: Wacky Wicker Workers

☐ **25 Smoking Stand,** white,
metal ashtray includes
matchbox holder and
match striker,
c 1920's . . **110.00 140.00**
Credit: House of Wicker

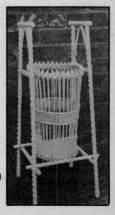

☐ **26 Umbrella Stand,** white,
unique stand is wrapped
with wide binder cane,
c 1920's . . **175.00 250.00**
Credit: Wacky Wicker Workers

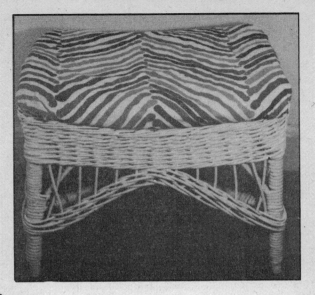

STOOLS

☐ **1 Footstool,** white, made of reed, c 1920's **90.00**   **135.00**
   Credit: The Wicker Lady

☐ **2 Footstool,** white, spring construction, newly up-
   holstered cushion, c 1920's **125.00**   **150.00**
   Credit: The Collected Works

☐ **3 Shoe Store Stool,** white, rare, Bar Harbor design on sides, six legs, made of fiber, c 1920's . **150.00   225.00**
Credit: Lightfoot House

TABLES

☐ **1 Dining Table,** white, solid wood top is 42″ in diameter, closely woven skirting under top and on base, brass tips on feet, c 1920's **300.00   475.00**
Credit: Wacky Wicker Workers

☐ **2 End Table,** natural finish, made of fiber, oak top is 12″ in diameter, brass foot caps,
c 1920's . . **135.00 165.00**
Credit: The Collected Works

☐ **3 End Table,** white, made of fiber by the Lloyd loom, Heywood-Wakefield Company,
c 1920's . . **135.00 200.00**
Credit: Windsor's Cane & Wicker Repair

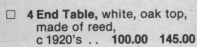

☐ **4 End Table,** white, oak top, made of reed,
c 1920's . . **100.00 145.00**

☐ **6 Library Table,** white, oak top is 42" long, closely woven reed bottom shelf, c 1920's .. **275.00   350.00**
Credit: Montgomery Auction Exchange

☐ **5 Gateleg Table,** white, rare, three-piece oak top folds down for easy storage, top is 42" in diameter when extended, oak bottom shelf, handmade wickerwork is woven from reed, c 1920's .. **575.00   700.00**
Credit: House of Wicker

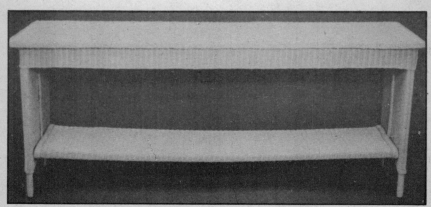

☐ **7 Library Table,** white, rare, 6' long, machine-made wickerwork made by the Lloyd loom, closely woven top and bottom shelf, Heywood-Wakefield Company. **400.00   550.00**
Credit: The Wicker Garden

☐ **8 Library Table,** white, solid
  wood top and bottom
  shelf, made of fiber, six
  legs,
  c 1925 . . . .   **350.00   425.00**

☐ **9 Oblong Table,** white, 36″
  long, closely woven skirting, made of reed,
  c 1920's . . **285.00   375.00**
*Credit: Montgomery Auction
Exchange*

☐ **10 Oblong Table,** white, oval
  oak top 36″ in diameter,
  handmade of fiber, painted
  oval bottom shelf, six legs,
  c 1920's . . **475.00   550.00**

☐ **11 Oblong Table,** white, oval oak top, rectangular bottom shelf, wickerwork woven by machine, c 1920's .. **275.00** **350.00**

☐ **12 Oval Table,** natural finish, oak top is 26″ long, c 1920's .. **225.00** **300.00**
Credit: Wisteria Antiques

☐ **13 Oval Table,** natural finish, 38″ long, oak top has beveled edges and highly unique shape, c 1920's **500.00** **625.00**
Credit: Cubbyhole Antiques

☐ **14 Oval Table,** painted black
and brown, diamond design
woven into fiber skirting
and touched with black
paint, solid wood top,
c 1920's . . **250.00 350.00**
Credit: Bale Mill Inn & Antiques

☐ **15 Magazine Table,** white,
rare, closely woven top
and bottom shelf, one
drawer, double-basket
magazine holders,
c 1920's . . **325.00 400.00**
Credit: Cubbyhole Antiques

☐ **16 Round Table,** natural
finish, oak centers and
turned wood frame,
circular wickerwork,
c 1920's . . **150.00 225.00**
Credit: Wacky Wicker Workers

☐ **17 Round Table,** white, oak top, combination oak and fiber bottom shelf, c 1920's .. **185.00 275.00**
Credit: Wacky Wicker Workers

☐ **18 Round Table,** white, oak top is 15″ in diameter, reed skirting and cane-wrapped legs, c 1920's .. **150.00 225.00**

☐ **19 Round Table,** white, willow, circular-woven two tier design, twisted willow ball feet, c 1920's .. **160.00 200.00**

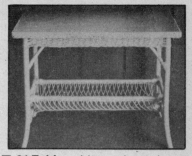

☐ **21 Table,** white, oak top is
26″ long,
V-shaped woven book
stand below, made of fiber,
c 1920's .. **145.00   190.00**

☐ **20 Square Table,** natural
finish, woven reed top and
bottom shelf,
c 1920's .. **200.00   275.00**

☐ **22 Tall Side Table,** natural finish, oak top is 20″ in
diameter, handmade of reed, diamond design
set into closely woven base, c 1920's **500.00   650.00**
Credit: Cubbyhole Antiques

TEA CARTS

☐ **1 Tea Cart,** brown, lift-off
glass tray, bottom shelf,
two drawers,
c 1920's . . **425.00 550.00**

☐ **2 Tea Cart,** natural finish,
lift-off tray, two serving
shelves, wooden wheels,
handmade of fiber,
c 1920's . . **400.00 500.00**
*Credit: Montgomery Auction
Exchange*

☐ **3 Tea Cart,** white, closely woven top and bottom
shelf of reed, c 1920's **325.00   450.00**
Credit: Montgomery Auction Exchange

☐ **4 Tea Cart,** natural finish,
rare, lift-off oval tray,
turned wood handle, oval
bottom shelf,
c 1920's . . **425.00   575.00**
Credit: The Collected Works

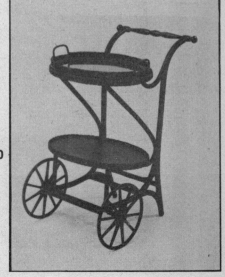

☐ **5 Tea Cart,** white, lift-off woven tray, two shelves
below, c 1920's 450.00   525.00
Credit: Gibson-Girl Memories

☐ **6 Tea Cart,** white, glass top, two square glass-
topped shelves, wood wheels, thick braidwork
on top, c 1920's 500.00   650.00
Credit: Cubbyhole Antiques

MISCELLANEOUS

☐ **1 Baby Carriage,** white, classic Lloyd loom design, made by machine with fiber, rubber tires, adjustable hood, c 1920's **285.00**   **385.00**

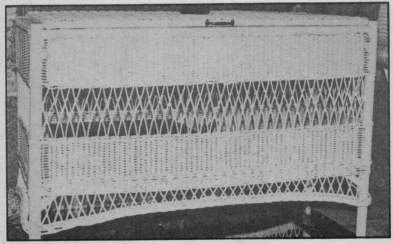

☐ **2 Blanket Chest,** white, 43″ long, handmade of reed, hinged lid with brass handle, c 1920's . . .   **350.00**   **500.00**

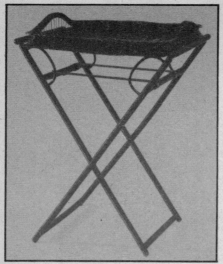

☐ **3 Butler's Tray,** natural finish, glass-topped tray lifts off, made of reed, turned wood legs, c 1920's .. **125.00 175.00**
Credit: Heirloom Wicker

☐ **4 China Cabinet,** white, center glass door, two front and two side glass panels, c 1920's .. **2500.00 +**
Credit: A Summer Place

□ **6 Candlestick Holders,**
natural finish, 5″ high,
closely woven reed,
wooden bases,
c 1920's .. **40.00   60.00**
Credit: The Collected Works

□ **5 China Cabinet, white, rare,**
64″ high, diamond design
woven into top trim, single
drawer, braidwork frames,
cabinet door,
c 1920's .. **2200.00 +**
Credit: The Wicker Garden

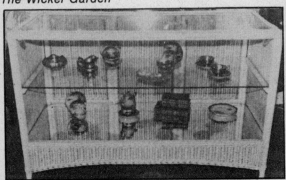

□ **7 Display Case, white, extremely rare, 3 feet tall**
and 5 feet long, two hinged wicker panels open
in back section for easy access, glass shelves,
c 1920's .... **1800.00 +**
Credit: Arabesque Antiques

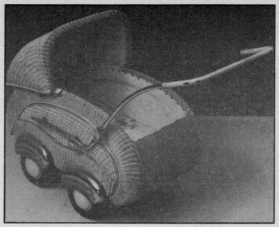

☐ **8 Doll Buggy,** white, rare, Art Deco style, chrome
fenders, made by machine with fiber, c 1925 ...   200.00   350.00
Credit: The Collected Works

☐ **9 Dresser,** white, four drawers, glass pulls, wrapped ball feet on casters, c 1920's 900.00   1400.00

☐ **10 Dressing Screen,** white, rare, made of fiber, three panels covered in blue material, c 1920's .   **300.00   450.00**

☐ **11 Electric Fountain,** white,
very rare, gold mood lamp
in center, metal liner,
woven side pockets for
plants, handmade of fiber,
often used in hotel lobbies
and restaurants,
c. 1920's . . **300.00   500.00**
Credit: The Wicker Lady

☐ **12 Fireside Bench,** natural finish, rare, closely
woven skirting, six-legged design, c 1920's **225.00   325.00**
Credit: A Summer Place

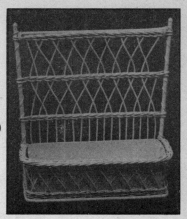

☐ 13 Hanging Planter, white,
designed for use on a wall,
metal liner, wood and reed
construction,
c 1920's .. **50.00 75.00**
Credit: The Collected Works

☐ 14 Hassock, white,
upholstered lift-top for
storage or could be used
as a hamper,
c 1920's .. **125.00 200.00**
Credit: The Wicker Garden

☐ 15 Inkwell Holder, rare,
painted green, wooden
base, scalloped reed trim,
c 1920's .. **100.00 150.00**
Credit: The Collected Works

Round Lake Antiques

WE BUY AND SELL OLD WICKER FURNITURE

- **ANTIQUE WICKER**

- **RESTORATION**

Owners Dottie and Ken Thompson
carry a large inventory of wicker dating from
the late 1800s to the 1930s. They also
specialize in in-house repairs assuring the
customer of fine condition and quality.

Round Lake Antiques
Box 358, Route 9
Round Lake, NY 12151

Tel. (518) 899-2394

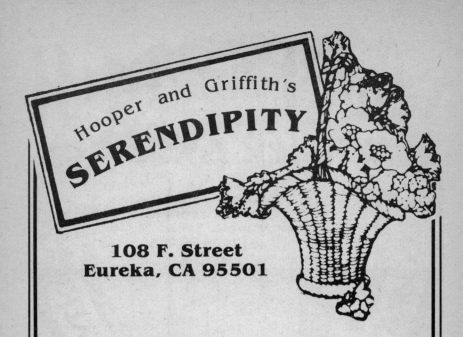

**29 WHITFIELD STREET
GUILFORD, CT 06437**

(203) 453-5153

HOURS BY APPOINTMENT

Mary Jean McLaughlin

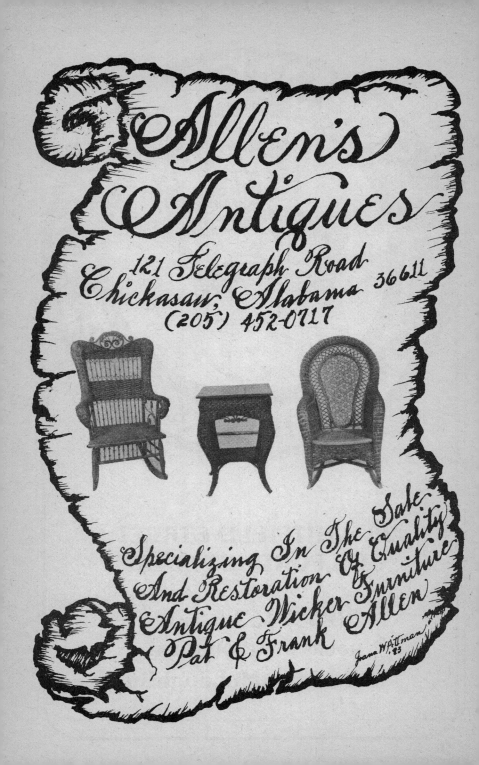

WICKERING HEIGHTS

Fine Antique Wicker —
Bought and Sold

home of "THE WICKER WIZARD"
EXPERT RESTORATION
Victorian a Specialty

415 Superior Street
Rossford, Ohio 43460
(419) 666-9461

The Wicker Garden

1318 Madison Avenue   New York City 10028
212-348-1166

Wacky Wicker Workers

Jim & Marian
of
Mentor
Ohio

255-1172

Appraise • Buy • Sell • Restore

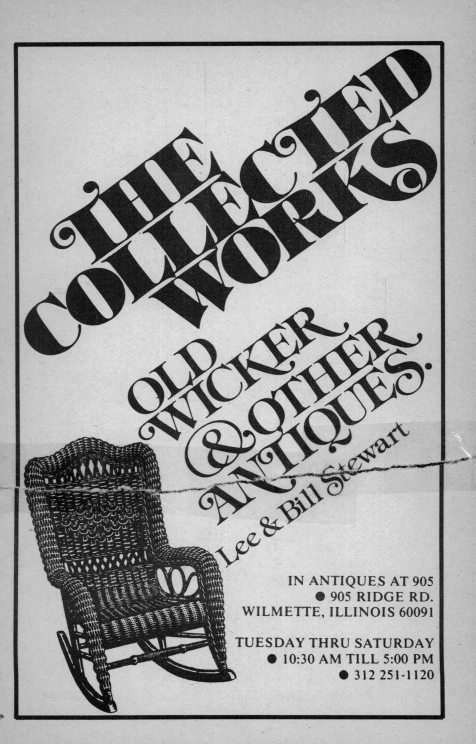

THE OFFICIAL PRICE GUIDES TO:

☐ 465-8 **American Silver & Silver Plate** 4th Ed.	10.95
☐ 482-8 **Antique Clocks** 3rd Ed.	10.95
☐ 283-3 **Antique & Modern Dolls** 3rd Ed.	10.95
☐ 287-6 **Antique & Modern Firearms** 6th Ed.	11.95
☐ 271-X **Antiques & Other Collectibles** 6th Ed.	9.95
☐ 289-2 **Antique Jewelry** 5th Ed.	11.95
☐ 270-1 **Beer Cans & Collectibles,** 3rd Ed.	7.95
☐ 262-0 **Bottles Old & New** 9th Ed.	10.95
☐ 255-8 **Carnival Glass** 1st Ed.	10.95
☐ 453-4 **Collectible Cameras** 2nd Ed.	10.95
☐ 277-9 **Collectibles of the Third Reich** 2nd Ed.	10.95
☐ 281-7 **Collectible Toys** 3rd Ed.	10.95
☐ 490-9 **Collector Cars** 6th Ed.	11.95
☐ 267-1 **Collector Handguns** 3rd Ed.	11.95
☐ 290-6 **Collector Knives** 8th Ed.	11.95
☐ 266-3 **Collector Plates** 4th Ed.	11.95
☐ 476-3 **Collector Prints** 6th Ed.	11.95
☐ 489-5 **Comic Books & Collectibles** 8th Ed.	9.95
☐ 433-X **Depression Glass** 1st Ed.	9.95
☐ 472-0 **Glassware** 2nd Ed.	10.95
☐ 492-5 **Hummel Figurines & Plates** 5th Ed.	9.95
☐ 451-8 **Kitchen Collectibles** 2nd Ed.	10.95
☐ 291-4 **Military Collectibles** 5th Ed.	11.95
☐ 268-X **Music Collectibles** 5th Ed.	11.95
☐ 491-7 **Old Books & Autographs** 6th Ed.	10.95
☐ 298-1 **Oriental Collectibles** 3rd Ed.	11.95
☐ 297-3 **Paper Collectibles** 5th Ed.	10.95
☐ 276-0 **Pottery & Porcelain** 5th Ed.	11.95
☐ 263-9 **Radio, T.V. & Movie Memorabilia** 2nd Ed.	11.95
☐ 288-4 **Records** 7th Ed.	10.95
☐ 485-2 **Royal Doulton** 4th Ed.	10.95
☐ 280-4 **Science Fiction & Fantasy Collectibles** 2nd Ed.	10.95
☐ 477-1 **Wicker** 3rd Ed.	10.95

THE OFFICIAL:

☐ 445-3 **Collector's Journal** 1st Ed.	4.95
☐ 365-1 **Encyclopedia of Antiques** 1st Ed.	9.95
☐ 369-4 **Guide to Buying & Selling Antiques** 1st Ed.	9.95
☐ 414-3 **Identification Guide to Early American Furniture** 1st Ed.	9.95
☐ 413-5 **Identification Guide to Glassware** 1st Ed.	9.95
☐ 448-8 **Identification Guide to Gunmarks** 2nd Ed.	9.95
☐ 412-7 **Identification Guide to Pottery & Porcelain** 1st Ed.	9.95
☐ 415-1 **Identification Guide to Victorian Furniture** 1st Ed.	9.95

THE OFFICIAL (POCKET SIZE) PRICE GUIDES TO:

☐ 473-9 **Antiques & Flea Markets** 3rd Ed.	3.95
☐ 442-9 **Antique Jewelry** 2nd Ed.	3.95
☐ 264-7 **Baseball Cards** 5th Ed.	4.95
☐ 488-7 **Bottles** 2nd Ed.	4.95
☐ 468-2 **Cars & Trucks** 2nd Ed.	4.95
☐ 260-4 **Collectible Americana** 1st Ed.	4.95
☐ 294-9 **Collectible Records** 3rd Ed.	4.95
☐ 469-0 **Collector Guns** 2nd Ed.	4.95
☐ 474-7 **Comic Books** 3rd Ed.	3.95
☐ 486-0 **Dolls** 3rd Ed.	4.95
☐ 292-2 **Football Cards** 5th Ed.	4.95
☐ 258-2 **Glassware** 2nd Ed.	4.95
☐ 487-9 **Hummels** 3rd Ed.	4.95
☐ 441-0 **Military Collectibles** 2nd Ed.	3.95
☐ 480-1 **Paperbacks & Magazines** 3rd Ed.	4.95
☐ 443-7 **Pocket Knives** 2nd Ed.	3.95
☐ 479-8 **Scouting Collectibles** 3rd Ed.	4.95
☐ 439-9 **Sports Collectibles** 2nd Ed.	3.95
☐ 494-1 **Star Trek/Star Wars Collectibles** 3rd Ed.	3.95
☐ 493-3 **Toys** 3rd Ed.	4.95

THE OFFICIAL BLACKBOOK PRICE GUIDES OF:

☐ 284-1 **U.S. Coins** 24th Ed.	3.95
☐ 286-8 **U.S. Paper Money** 18th Ed.	3.95
☐ 285-X **U.S. Postage Stamps** 8th Ed.	3.95

THE OFFICIAL INVESTORS GUIDE TO BUYING & SELLING:

☐ 496-8 **Gold, Silver and Diamonds** 2nd Ed.	9.95
☐ 497-6 **Gold Coins** 2nd Ed.	9.95
☐ 498-4 **Silver Coins** 2nd Ed.	9.95
☐ 499-2 **Silver Dollars** 2nd Ed.	9.95

THE OFFICIAL NUMISMATIC GUIDE SERIES:

☐ 481-X **Coin Collecting** 3rd Ed.	9.95
☐ 254-X **The Official Guide to Detecting Counterfeit Money** 2nd Ed.	7.95
☐ 257-4 **The Official Guide to Mint Errors** 4th Ed.	7.95
☐ 256-6 **The Official Hewitt-Donlon Price Guide to Small Size Paper Money** 15th Ed.	7.95
☐ 162-4 **Variety & Oddity Guide of U.S. Coins** 8th Ed.	4.95

SPECIAL INTEREST SERIES:

☐ 506-9 **From Hearth to Cookstove** 3rd Ed.	17.95
☐ 370-8 **Lucky Number Lottery Guide** 1st Ed.	3.50
☐ 504-2 **On Method Acting** 8th Printing	6.95

TOTAL	

FOR IMMEDIATE DELIVERY

VISA & MASTER CARD CUSTOMERS

ORDER TOLL FREE!
1-800-638-6460

This number is for orders only; it is not tied into the customer service or business office. Customers not using charge cards must use mail for ordering since payment is required with the order — sorry no C.O.D.'s.

OR SEND ORDERS TO ▮ ▮ ▮ ▮ ▮

THE HOUSE OF COLLECTIBLES, *201 East 50th Street*
New York, New York 10022

┌─ POSTAGE & HANDLING RATE CHART ─┐

TOTAL ORDER/POSTAGE	TOTAL ORDER/POSTAGE	
0 to $10.00 - **$1.25**	$20.01 to $30.00 - **$2.00**	**$50.01 & Over -**
$10.01 to $20.00 - **$1.60**	$30.01 to $40.00 - **$2.75**	**Add 10% of your total order**
	$40.01 to $50.00 - **$3.50**	(Ex. $75.00 x .10 = $7.50)

Total from columns on reverse side. Quantity_____ $ _____

[ ] Check or money order enclosed $_____ (include postage and handling)

[ ] Please charge $_____ to my: [ ] MASTERCARD [ ] VISA

Charge Card Customers Not Using Our Toll Free Number Please Fill Out The Information Below.

Account No. (All Digits) _____ Expiration Date _____

Signature_____

NAME (please print) _____ PHONE _____

ADDRESS _____ APT. # _____

CITY _____ STATE _____ ZIP _____